Surviving the Embrace

Surviving the Embrace

Matthew Petchinsky

Surviving the Embrace: The Ultimate Guide to Encounters with The Hugging Molly

By: Matthew Petchinsky

Introduction to The Hugging Molly Survival Guide

The night is a time when shadows stretch long, sounds deepen, and ancient legends seem to come alive. Among these tales, few are as haunting as the legend of The Hugging Molly—a figure known for her startling, intense nighttime encounters that have struck fear into communities for generations. Often depicted as a towering woman, shrouded in darkness, with arms outstretched, she is said to seek out those who dare to wander alone after dark. Her chilling embrace, a firm yet ghostly hug, is reputed to leave her victims shaken, their ears ringing from her bone-chilling scream. But what drives The Hugging Molly? What lies beneath her spectral presence, and how can one hope to survive an encounter with this fearsome figure? This guide will explore these questions and more, preparing readers with both knowledge and strategies to face the unknown.

The Legend of The Hugging Molly

The Hugging Molly is more than just a ghost story whispered in the dark—she is a piece of living folklore, her legend passed down through generations. Stories about her vary across regions, but the essence remains the same: a tall woman, dressed in black, who roams the lonely streets at night, especially in isolated rural areas. She is not known for causing physical harm, but her intense hug and ear-piercing scream leave a lasting impact on those she encounters. Unlike other spirits or entities that shy away from human contact, The Hugging Molly seems driven by a deep, inexplicable need to approach and embrace those she finds wandering alone, often leaving them with an unsettling sense of dread that lingers long after the encounter.

Historical and Cultural Background

The origins of The Hugging Molly are murky, steeped in mystery and varied across cultures. In some regions, she is seen as a guardian, frightening children indoors to protect them from real-life dangers lurking in the night. In others, she is a ghostly reminder of loss or sorrow, a mother who lost her child and now seeks to hold others close in her unending grief. Some believe she is a warning or a messenger, while others consider her a restless spirit, cursed to wander until she finds peace.

Across various cultures, The Hugging Molly embodies a universal archetype: the eerie, otherworldly figure who unsettles and confounds. Her legend is woven with elements of both fear and sympathy, for she is not wholly malevolent. She seeks to frighten, yes, but also to connect, in her own terrifying way. Understanding her origins and the contexts in which her legend grew offers insight into her actions and intentions—insights that may prove valuable in anticipating and surviving an encounter with her.

Purpose and Intent of the Guide

This guide serves a crucial purpose: to equip you with the knowledge, understanding, and survival strategies necessary to face The Hugging Molly should you ever encounter her. While it is impossible to know for certain when or where she might appear, or what might trigger her approach, preparation is key. By delving into her history, understanding her motivations, and learning proven techniques for avoiding or surviving her embrace, you will be empowered to face the unknown with resilience.

Our intent is not only to prepare you for a potential encounter but to deepen your understanding of the lore surrounding The Hugging Molly. Legends like hers endure because they tap into primal fears and emotions. By exploring her story in detail, we aim to demystify her presence and make it possible for readers to approach her legend with both respect and preparedness.

Tips for Utilizing This Guide

To make the most of this guide, keep the following tips in mind:

1. **Read with an Open Mind:** The Hugging Molly's legend contains elements of both superstition and historical truth. Approach each chapter with a willingness to consider multiple perspectives, as understanding the nuances of her story can be invaluable.

2. **Focus on the Practical Advice:** While the historical and cultural background offers essential context, survival requires practical strategies. Pay close attention to the recommended actions and precautions in the later chapters, as these may make the difference in avoiding or surviving a nighttime encounter.

3. **Stay Observant and Cautious:** Even if you believe that an encounter with The Hugging Molly is unlikely, remember that her legend serves as a reminder of the hidden dangers of the night. Use this guide as a tool to enhance your awareness and vigilance, especially when alone after dark.

4. **Engage with the Stories:** Throughout this guide, you'll find anecdotes and accounts from those who claim to have met The Hugging Molly. These stories are more than just tales—they hold potential clues and lessons. Treat them as firsthand insights into what might happen and consider how you would react in each scenario.

5. **Be Prepared but Not Fearful:** The Hugging Molly is a figure of fear, but this guide aims to replace fear with knowledge and preparation. Use what you learn here to feel more secure and grounded, knowing that you have equipped yourself with everything possible to face her if the time comes.

In the pages that follow, you will find a blend of history, culture, and survival tactics designed to offer you a comprehensive understanding of The Hugging Molly. Embrace the journey and remember: to face the unknown, one must first seek to understand it.

Chapter 1: Origins of The Hugging Molly Legend

The tale of The Hugging Molly is one shrouded in darkness and whispered through generations, a legend that has captivated communities and mystified folklorists alike. She has become synonymous with cautionary tales about the dangers of the night, a spectral figure both feared and revered. Understanding her origins requires a journey into the past, where historical accounts, regional folklore, and retellings across time have shaped her story into the haunting figure she is today. This chapter dives deep into the historical roots of The Hugging Molly, examining early sightings, analyzing regional variations, and exploring the possible inspirations behind this eerie legend.

Historical Accounts and Sightings

The Hugging Molly's story first appeared in recorded history in the late 1800s, primarily within small rural communities. Descriptions of her varied, but one thread remained consistent: she was a towering figure, clad in black, who would seize lone travelers or children wandering after dark, pulling them into a crushing embrace accompanied by an ear-piercing scream. Early reports emphasized her ominous yet oddly protective nature, suggesting that her embrace, though terrifying, was somehow rooted in concern for those she startled.

Several early accounts come from Alabama, where The Hugging Molly was believed to roam rural roads near small towns. One of the most notable records is a report from 1893, where a young farmhand recounted a harrowing experience: he claimed to have been grabbed from behind while walking home one night, unable to see his assailant but feeling the suffocating pressure of her grip and hearing her scream reverberate through the stillness. When he broke free, he turned only to find an empty road, yet the memory of her grip stayed with him for years. Similar accounts emerged in surrounding areas, building a reputation for The Hugging Molly as a silent guardian of the night who used fear to keep individuals from wandering alone.

Over the decades, sightings of The Hugging Molly continued to be reported sporadically, with peaks occurring during times of hardship or tension, such as the Great Depression and the post-WWII era. Many believe that the legend of The Hugging Molly intensified during these periods as communities sought symbols of caution and protection amid uncertainty. Each account, while unique in details, contributed to the mosaic of The Hugging Molly's identity, solidifying her role in local lore as a being both fearsome and strangely protective.

Regional Folklore and the Evolution of Molly's Story

The Hugging Molly's legend is not confined to one region or culture; rather, it has evolved and adapted as it traveled across various communities. In the southern United States, where the tale seems to have originated, she is often portrayed as a protective yet terrifying figure—a warning to children to come home before dark and a reminder of the unseen dangers that lurk in the quiet of night. Her story was commonly told to children by parents and grandparents as a cautionary tale to prevent them from wandering after dark.

In other parts of the country, however, her story took on additional layers. Some communities began to incorporate elements of local superstition, casting her as a vengeful spirit of a grieving mother or a tragic figure bound by a curse. For instance, in parts of Texas, The Hugging Molly was believed to be the ghost of a woman who had lost her family in a tragic accident, and now, unable to find peace, she wanders in search of others to "protect" in her own harrowing way. This variation of the tale added a sense of tragic empathy, transforming her from a mere frightening figure into a being driven by loss and sorrow.

As her legend spread, the Hugging Molly became an amalgamation of regional fears, beliefs, and cultural values. In northern states, some retellings cast her as a banshee-like figure, foretelling misfortune or danger to those who encountered her. This version retained the eerie, protective embrace but added an ominous layer, suggesting that her appearance heralded trouble for those she visited. The regional evolution of The Hugging Molly's legend speaks to the adaptability of folklore, as each culture and community imbued her with traits that resonated with their unique fears and values.

Analysis of Primary Sources and Retellings

Understanding The Hugging Molly's origins requires sifting through a range of primary sources, including newspaper articles, oral histories, and early folklore collections. Analysis of these sources reveals the complexities and variations in her legend, offering insight into how and why she evolved over time.

Newspaper articles from the late 19th and early 20th centuries occasionally reported mysterious sightings, often framing them as supernatural encounters that defied logical explanation. These reports, while sensationalized, provide some of the earliest written accounts of The Hugging Molly, preserving details of her appearance, behavior, and the emotions she stirred in witnesses. One article from 1901 described her as "an apparition that holds those she finds in a vice-like grip, echoing the night with a scream that can chill the bones." Such early descriptions highlight the consistent themes of her physical power and vocal terror, elements that have remained central to her legend.

Oral histories provide another rich vein of primary source material. Passed down through families and communities, these stories capture the nuances of The Hugging Molly's encounters, often imbuing her with additional characteristics, such as a specific look or a sorrowful expression, that add depth to her identity. Retellings from different family lines often added unique details, such as the belief that she was a "spirit in search of those who were lost." This personalization of the story created variations within local communities, contributing to the ever-evolving tapestry of her myth.

Finally, early folklore collections, compiled by researchers and historians, provide a structured analysis of The Hugging Molly legend. These collections often include theories about her origins, linking her to broader cultural archetypes, such as the guardian spirit, the mourning mother, or the vengeful wraith. Some folklorists suggest that The Hugging Molly may have been inspired by older European legends brought over by settlers, adapting into new forms in the American South. For example, her spectral embrace and haunting scream bear similarities to tales of banshees or other protective-yet-frightening figures from Irish folklore.

Through these sources, it becomes evident that The Hugging Molly is more than a single story; she is a compilation of regional fears, historical circumstances, and evolving cultural beliefs. Her legend has been shaped by those who encountered her, feared her, and perhaps even found solace in her terrifying presence. By tracing her origins through these primary accounts and retellings, we gain a clearer picture of why The Hugging Molly endures in the collective imagination and why her story continues to captivate and unsettle those who hear it.

In the chapters that follow, we will continue to explore her legend, delving into the ways in which her story has impacted communities, inspired cautionary practices, and left a lasting imprint on the folklore of those who believe in her. As we journey deeper into the world of The Hugging Molly, keep in mind the historical threads that connect her to the fears, hopes, and beliefs of generations past.

Chapter 2: Psychological Profile of The Hugging Molly

Understanding The Hugging Molly requires a blend of psychological interpretation and folklore analysis, examining her possible motives, behavioral patterns, and the common triggers that seem to draw her out of the shadows. In this chapter, we delve into her psychology, seeking to understand the intentions behind her seemingly contradictory actions. The Hugging Molly is at once a fearsome figure and a protective force, her spectral presence as unsettling as it is captivating. By piecing together the psychological and mythological dimensions of her legend, we can begin to unravel the mysteries surrounding her motives, behavior, and triggers.

Possible Motives and Behavioral Patterns

From the historical accounts and regional folklore discussed in the previous chapter, we know that The Hugging Molly's actions typically follow a distinct behavioral pattern: she approaches those wandering alone at night, envelops them in a constricting embrace, and emits an ear-piercing scream before vanishing. Though she does not harm her victims physically, her grip is suffocating, and her scream is said to resonate long after she disappears. Her behavior raises several questions: Why does she approach people alone? Why does she embrace them with such intensity, yet refrain from causing injury? To gain insight into her possible motives, let's examine her actions through various psychological lenses.

1. **Protective Instincts:** One common interpretation is that The Hugging Molly acts from a distorted sense of protection. Her approach often appears targeted at individuals who are alone, particularly children or young adults who are out after dark. Some folklorists suggest that The Hugging Molly's embrace is intended to keep her victims from harm, using fear as a method to deter them from wandering alone. This protective theory aligns with

certain maternal archetypes in folklore—figures who, though frightening, act out of concern for the safety of others. Her scream, under this interpretation, serves as both a warning and a reminder of the dangers lurking in the night, an auditory cue designed to instill caution.

2. **Expression of Grief or Loss:** Another possible motive lies in unresolved grief. In several regional versions of her story, The Hugging Molly is said to be the spirit of a mother who lost her child under tragic circumstances, such as illness, accident, or violence. Her intense hug and piercing scream might be manifestations of her unending sorrow, a desperate attempt to connect with others in a world where she feels alone. This interpretation frames her actions as those of a restless spirit, unable to process her grief, reaching out to fill an emotional void. Each hug becomes an attempt to reclaim the closeness she lost, and each scream an expression of her inconsolable pain.

3. **Desire for Control or Authority:** A darker interpretation of her motives suggests a psychological need for control. The Hugging Molly may use fear and physical dominance to exert authority over those who wander alone, a symbolic reclaiming of power. In this reading, her hug is less a form of connection and more an exertion of control, a way of asserting her presence and dominance over those who challenge the rules she has come to enforce. The scream, in this view, acts as a reinforcement of her authority, designed to shock and disorient, leaving a lasting impression on those she encounters.

4. **Compulsion or Obligation:** Some legends hint that The Hugging Molly may be driven by an external compulsion—a curse, punishment, or moral obligation that forces her to seek out and "warn" others through her fearsome embrace. In this interpretation, she might act not out of personal desire, but from an imposed duty to scare others into staying safe at night. This motivation could explain her consistent behavioral pattern; she may

feel bound by an unseen force or rule, compelled to repeat the same actions until her purpose is fulfilled or her curse is lifted.

Psychological Interpretations and Folklore Analysis

Folklorists and psychologists often explore legends like The Hugging Molly to understand the social and psychological needs they fulfill in communities. Figures such as Molly are not merely frightening entities; they are reflections of collective fears, societal norms, and deep-rooted psychological themes. Analyzing The Hugging Molly through this lens provides insights into the ways her legend addresses fundamental human anxieties, especially those surrounding isolation, safety, and the unknown.

1. **The Maternal Archetype in Folklore:** The Hugging Molly fits within a common archetype in folklore—the protective yet fearsome maternal figure. Characters who embody this archetype are often driven by a deep love or protective instinct, but they express it in unsettling ways, such as through intimidating warnings or supernatural interventions. In psychological terms, this figure represents a powerful, protective force that is simultaneously nurturing and terrifying, embodying both safety and fear. The Hugging Molly's behavior aligns with this archetype, suggesting that her legend serves as a cautionary tale and a symbol of maternal protection twisted by grief or duty.

2. **Projection of Societal Fears:** Legends like The Hugging Molly emerge in response to societal anxieties, often embodying fears that are too abstract to express directly. Her legend taps into primal fears of being alone, vulnerable, or unprotected in the darkness. For communities, especially those in rural or isolated areas, The Hugging Molly represents the dangers of the unknown—the lurking threats in the dark that could come from animals, strangers, or even supernatural forces. By personifying these fears in The Hugging Molly, communities give form to the otherwise

formless anxieties, creating a figure who symbolizes caution and protection against the perils of the night.

3. **Ambiguity as a Psychological Device:** One of the reasons The Hugging Molly's story endures is its inherent ambiguity. Her motives, origins, and intentions are never fully explained, which creates a sense of mystery and heightens her psychological impact. This ambiguity allows for multiple interpretations, making her a figure who can embody different fears and messages depending on the listener's perspective. Psychologically, this ambiguity plays on the human tendency to fear the unknown; by leaving her motives uncertain, her legend taps into our deepest anxieties about unpredictability and uncontrollable forces.

4. **The Cathartic Role of Fear:** Encountering The Hugging Molly, either through stories or alleged sightings, provides a form of catharsis. By experiencing fear in a controlled way—through the legend rather than a real encounter—individuals can confront and process their anxieties in a safe context. This cathartic role reinforces the value of The Hugging Molly's story, making her both a terrifying figure and a means of processing fear within the community.

Common Triggers for Her Appearances

While legends of The Hugging Molly's appearances vary, certain patterns and triggers seem to recur in stories, suggesting that specific circumstances might prompt her approach. Understanding these triggers can be invaluable for those seeking to avoid an encounter or prepare themselves if they sense her presence.

1. **Isolation and Loneliness:** The most consistent trigger for The Hugging Molly's appearance is the state of being alone at night. Her legend is filled with accounts of individuals walking solitary roads or isolated paths who then experience her chilling embrace. This trigger suggests a connection to vulnerability; she seems drawn to those who are without companionship, perhaps sensing a need to protect, warn, or, in some cases, exert control over those who dare to travel alone.

2. **Disregard for Curfews or Warnings:** In some versions of her legend, The Hugging Molly appears to those who ignore community rules or curfews. Her appearance then acts as a supernatural reinforcement of these societal guidelines. By targeting those who defy the "safety of home," she embodies the consequences of recklessness or defiance. This trigger reinforces the notion of her as a cautionary figure, seeking to instill respect for safety through fear.

3. **Emotional Vulnerability or Grief:** Another commonly reported trigger is emotional distress or vulnerability. Stories tell of individuals who, grieving or troubled, encounter The Hugging Molly as if drawn by her own sorrow. This connection implies that her spirit might resonate with those experiencing similar emotions, perhaps recognizing a reflection of her own unresolved

pain. In these cases, her appearance may be less about warning and more about a need to connect with others who share her emotional state.

4. **Periods of Social or Community Tension:** Interestingly, sightings of The Hugging Molly often increase during times of social or community tension, such as economic hardship or public unrest. This pattern suggests that she may act as a communal manifestation of shared anxieties, her presence a symbol of the fears and uncertainties held by the community at large. During such times, her legend might serve to channel collective emotions, using her presence as a warning or reminder of the need for caution and unity.

By examining her motives, psychology, and triggers, we begin to see The Hugging Molly as more than just a spectral figure. She is a complex entity, a mirror reflecting both individual vulnerabilities and the broader social fears of the community. Her legend endures because it resonates with universal themes of protection, fear, and the unknown, offering a haunting reminder that the darkest shadows often hold more than meets the eye.

Chapter 3: Recognizing the Signs of Her Presence

The Hugging Molly's approach is often subtle at first, marked by a series of environmental and auditory cues that can be easily dismissed if one isn't attuned to her presence. Recognizing these signs may provide a crucial window of opportunity for those who find themselves alone at night, offering a chance to avoid a direct encounter with this mysterious figure. This chapter details the indicators that commonly precede The Hugging Molly's appearance, exploring both environmental and auditory warnings, the importance of her nighttime manifestations, and case studies that highlight early warning signs observed by those who claim to have encountered her.

Environmental Cues and Auditory Warnings

The Hugging Molly rarely appears without warning, and those who have encountered her often report specific environmental shifts and auditory signals that signal her impending presence. While these cues may vary depending on the individual and setting, certain patterns have emerged from reported sightings and folklore accounts, suggesting a predictable sequence of events that may allow one to anticipate her approach.

Environmental Cues

1. **Sudden Drop in Temperature:** One of the most commonly reported signs of The Hugging Molly's presence is a sudden, inexplicable drop in temperature. Witnesses describe feeling a bone-chilling cold that seems to seep into the air, regardless of the season or weather. This drop in temperature is often localized, affecting only the immediate area, and many describe it as an intense cold that feels unnaturally isolating. This cue is thought to reflect a supernatural presence, a shift in energy that serves as an unspoken warning of her arrival.

2. **Dense Fog or Mist:** In certain areas, particularly in rural or isolated locations, her appearance is often accompanied by a sudden

fog or mist. This mist may seem to roll in without warning, covering the ground and obscuring visibility, as if shielding her movements from view. This phenomenon, though not always present, is considered a strong indicator of her approach. Folklore suggests that the fog acts as a veil between the living and the supernatural, allowing The Hugging Molly to move unseen until she chooses to reveal herself.

3. **Sudden Silence in Nature:** A less obvious but significant environmental cue is the abrupt quieting of natural sounds. Birds stop chirping, insects cease their buzzing, and even the wind seems to still. This silence is particularly unsettling in rural areas, where ambient noises are common. Many who have encountered The Hugging Molly report that this silence acts as a precursor to her approach, as if the natural world is holding its breath in anticipation of her presence.

4. **Dark Shadows or Flickering Lights:** Witnesses frequently describe seeing shadows that appear to shift or move on their own. Streetlights may flicker or dim inexplicably, and light sources often seem unable to fully pierce the darkness. This unsettling phenomenon has been linked to The Hugging Molly's spectral nature, with some believing that she draws energy from her surroundings, affecting light sources and creating an aura of darkness.

Auditory Warnings

1. **Footsteps in the Distance:** One of the earliest auditory signs associated with The Hugging Molly's approach is the sound of footsteps. These footsteps are often faint and may seem to follow the individual at a distance, echoing in a way that makes it difficult to pinpoint their source. Many describe this sound as slow, deliberate steps, as if someone were pacing behind them, closing the distance gradually.

2. **Soft Whispers or Breathing:** Another commonly reported sound is a faint, almost inaudible whisper or the sensation of someone breathing nearby. These whispers are often indistinct, making it impossible to discern words, yet their presence is unmistakable. Witnesses frequently report feeling as though someone is watching them, as if they are not alone, even though no one is visible. This auditory cue tends to heighten the feeling of vulnerability and isolation, particularly when paired with the environmental cues described above.

3. **Distant Scream or Cry:** The Hugging Molly's scream is her most infamous auditory hallmark, and while it is typically heard up close, some have reported hearing a faint scream in the distance before she appears. This scream, even when distant, is described as chilling and blood-curdling, often echoing through the night air in a way that suggests it is both otherworldly and urgent. The sound of her scream is thought to be a warning, a signal of her presence, and a reminder of the fear she instills.

4. **The Sound of Rushing Wind:** A less common but significant auditory warning is the sound of a strong, sudden wind. Some who have encountered her describe hearing a gust of wind that seems to come from nowhere, rushing past them as if someone has moved close by. This phenomenon is often accompanied by

the feeling of a presence passing, leaving behind a sense of unease and anticipation.

The Significance of Nighttime Appearances

The Hugging Molly is known exclusively for her nighttime appearances, and the significance of this timing cannot be overlooked. Her manifestation under the cover of darkness is rooted in both psychological and cultural associations with the night. In folklore, nighttime is often symbolic of the unknown, a time when the boundaries between the physical and supernatural worlds blur, allowing spirits and otherworldly beings to roam freely.

1. **Psychological Vulnerability at Night:** Psychologically, nighttime evokes a sense of vulnerability and isolation, particularly in secluded or unfamiliar areas. The absence of light reduces visibility, heightens fear, and can lead individuals to feel more susceptible to unseen threats. The Hugging Molly's preference for night aligns with this inherent vulnerability, as her presence preys on the fear of the unknown, using darkness to heighten the tension and sense of dread.

2. **The Mystical and Symbolic Nature of Darkness:** In many cultures, nighttime represents a liminal space, a threshold between the living and the dead. Spirits and supernatural entities are believed to become active during this time, roaming freely in the absence of sunlight. By appearing only at night, The Hugging Molly's legend ties her to the mystical qualities of darkness, reinforcing her as a being from the other side—a figure who exists in the shadows, operating under rules that defy the logic of the waking world.

3. **Increased Sense of Isolation:** Encounters with The Hugging Molly often occur in isolated settings, such as empty roads, rural paths, or quiet neighborhoods. This isolation is amplified at night, when fewer people are around, creating an atmosphere in

which the individual is left truly alone. The significance of her nighttime appearances, therefore, is not merely practical but symbolic, as she seeks out those who wander into the emptiness and solitude of the dark.

Case Studies of Encounters and Early Warning Signs

Examining documented encounters with The Hugging Molly reveals valuable insights into her behavior and the early warning signs of her presence. These case studies highlight patterns and recurring themes that may aid in recognizing her approach.

Case Study 1: The Farmhand on Hollow Creek Road

In 1893, a young farmhand reported encountering The Hugging Molly while walking home late at night. According to his account, he first noticed a sudden chill in the air, despite the warm summer evening. As he continued down the dirt road, he heard faint footsteps behind him, though he could see no one when he turned. The surrounding fields seemed to go eerily quiet, the usual night sounds replaced by an unnatural silence. Moments later, he felt the distinct sensation of being watched, followed by the sound of breathing close by. Before he could react, she appeared, embracing him with an iron grip and screaming into his ear. His encounter highlights several key early warning signs: the temperature drop, footsteps, and the sensation of being watched—all indicators of her approach.

Case Study 2: The Widow on Moonlit Lane

In 1921, an elderly widow described encountering The Hugging Molly near her home on a secluded lane. She recounted feeling a strange compulsion to leave her house that night, drawn outside by an indescribable force. As she stepped onto her porch, she felt a sudden chill, followed by an unsettling silence. The trees seemed to cast unusually deep shadows, and the light from her lantern dimmed inexplicably. She then heard the faint sound of whispering, as if someone were speaking just beyond the reach of the light. The next moment, The Hugging Molly appeared, enveloping her in a tight embrace and screaming before vanishing into the darkness. This case underscores the significance of environmental cues such as shadowy surroundings, sudden silence, and inexplicable auditory phenomena.

Case Study 3: The Young Hiker in Misty Valley

In 1987, a young hiker reported an encounter with The Hugging Molly while camping in a remote area. He described hearing a distant scream that echoed through the valley, followed by a thick fog that rolled in, limiting his visibility. As he walked along the trail, he felt an overwhelming sense of dread, accompanied by a chill that seemed to penetrate through his clothes. Suddenly, he heard footsteps behind him and saw shadows shifting in the fog. Before he could react, The Hugging Molly appeared, pulling him into a hug that left him breathless, her scream reverberating through the mist. This encounter highlights additional signs such as dense fog, the distant scream, and the sensation of an unseen presence.

Summary of Recognizing Her Presence

The Hugging Molly's approach is marked by a series of environmental and auditory cues that, when recognized, may provide an opportunity to avoid a direct encounter. Her preference for nighttime, paired with environmental shifts and haunting sounds, creates an atmosphere designed to unsettle and disorient. By understanding these warning signs, one can increase their awareness and potentially evade her ghostly embrace.

Chapter 4: Preparing for a Potential Encounter

Confronting The Hugging Molly is no ordinary experience. For those who travel through her domain at night, preparation is crucial, as it can make the difference between a terrifying encounter and a successful escape. Preparing for an encounter involves more than carrying physical items; it requires cultivating a resilient mindset, emotional readiness, and calm, intentional actions. In this chapter, we will explore the essential tools and techniques that can help one face The Hugging Molly with courage and control, from practical items to carry to strategies for maintaining composure in the face of fear.

Essential Items to Carry

Preparation for a potential encounter with The Hugging Molly starts with packing essential items that can aid in defense, increase visibility, and provide a sense of security. Although these tools may not stop her entirely, they can create a buffer, giving you time to act or escape if needed.

1. Bright Flashlight

One of the most critical items to carry is a high-lumen flashlight. While The Hugging Molly is a spectral figure, stories often suggest that intense light can disrupt her approach, as she is most commonly associated with darkness and shadows. A flashlight can help you observe your surroundings, identify potential hiding spots, and deter her from approaching. In case of an encounter, shine the light directly in her direction to create a barrier of brightness between you and her, which may give you precious seconds to act.

2. Personal Alarm or Whistle

Auditory tools, such as personal alarms or whistles, can be effective in creating an immediate disruption. High-pitched sounds may act as a form of distraction, potentially unsettling her and diverting her attention. If you feel her presence, activate the alarm or blow the whistle to create noise and draw attention, as she tends to appear in isolated settings. This sound may help to keep you alert while signaling to anyone nearby that assistance is needed.

3. Protective Amulet or Charm

Throughout folklore, certain symbols or charms are thought to protect individuals from supernatural entities. Consider carrying a small protective amulet, such as one that holds personal or cultural significance. Some individuals choose charms with religious significance, such as a cross, while others may carry symbolic talismans that hold meaning to them personally. While there is no guarantee that these will deter The Hugging Molly, the psychological benefit of feeling protected can boost confidence, making it easier to maintain a calm mindset.

4. Journal and Pen

A less obvious but valuable tool is a small journal and pen. Carrying a journal allows you to note down any unusual signs or experiences, which can help you stay observant and focused. Writing down potential environmental cues, such as changes in temperature or sounds, can help you remain alert and provide a record of events should an encounter occur. Additionally, focusing on writing can be a grounding activity that helps to steady nerves and keep you from succumbing to panic.

5. Emergency Blanket

Encounters with The Hugging Molly are frequently associated with a sudden drop in temperature. An emergency blanket, which retains body heat, can protect against the cold and help maintain physical comfort, even in the midst of an encounter. Staying warm can also improve mental clarity, which is essential in high-stress situations.

6. Portable Mirror

Some legends suggest that mirrors can repel or reveal supernatural beings, reflecting what is otherwise invisible to the naked eye. Carrying a compact mirror can serve a dual purpose: it may provide a view of anything approaching from behind, and it can be used to "reflect" The Hugging Molly if she is close by. Although largely symbolic, mirrors have long been used as protection against spirits, and having one on hand can be an additional psychological shield against fear.

Mindset and Emotional Readiness

In addition to tangible items, one of the most critical aspects of preparation is developing the right mindset. Encounters with The Hugging Molly can be profoundly unsettling, and fear can quickly escalate if not kept in check. Building emotional resilience and mental readiness can help you face her calmly and respond strategically rather than reactively.

1. Cultivate Fear Management Techniques

Learning to manage fear is essential when preparing for a potential encounter. Practice deep-breathing exercises, such as the 4-7-8 method: inhale for four seconds, hold the breath for seven seconds, and exhale for eight seconds. This technique helps to regulate your heart rate and calm the nervous system. Practicing mindfulness meditation can also be beneficial, as it trains the mind to observe feelings of fear without succumbing to them.

2. Visualize the Encounter

Visualization can be a powerful tool for mental preparedness. Imagine encountering The Hugging Molly: visualize each potential sign of her presence and rehearse your response to each. Consider how you will feel, where you might move, and how you will use the tools you've prepared. This mental rehearsal not only reduces the element of surprise but also strengthens your ability to act rationally in the face of an encounter.

3. Acknowledge, Don't Dismiss, Fear

Rather than suppressing or ignoring fear, acknowledge it as a natural reaction to an extraordinary situation. Fear is a survival mechanism, and recognizing its presence allows you to work with it rather than against it. By acknowledging your fear, you prevent it from overwhelming your rational mind, making it easier to focus on the steps needed to ensure safety.

4. Practice Grounding Techniques

Grounding techniques can help you remain focused and present, preventing your mind from spiraling into panic. Techniques such as the "5-4-3-2-1" method—identifying five things you see, four things you can touch, three things you hear, two things you can smell, and one thing you can taste—are useful in high-stress moments. Grounding keeps your mind engaged with the present, reducing the risk of dissociation or overwhelming fear.

How to Anticipate and Act Calmly

A calm mind and calculated actions are vital during an encounter. By staying attuned to her signs and practicing measured responses, you increase your chances of avoiding an intense encounter and minimizing her impact.

1. Observe Your Surroundings

The first step to acting calmly is staying observant. Pay close attention to any environmental changes, such as shifts in temperature or silence in nature. Keep your flashlight ready, and scan your surroundings periodically to ensure you're aware of any unusual movement. This proactive approach prevents you from being caught off-guard and allows you to assess whether The Hugging Molly may be near.

2. Maintain a Slow and Steady Pace

If you sense her presence, avoid running or making sudden movements, as this may trigger her attention. Instead, maintain a slow, steady pace and avoid looking directly into the darkness. Many reports suggest that The Hugging Molly is more likely to approach if you display signs of panic, as she seems drawn to fear and vulnerability. Moving at a controlled pace can help you conserve energy, keep your wits about you, and avoid escalating the situation.

3. Use Auditory Distractions

If you hear footsteps or whispers, consider using your personal alarm or whistle as a deterrent. These noises can create an interruption in her approach, giving you time to put distance between you and her. Auditory distractions may help to disorient her, reducing her hold over the atmosphere and allowing you to regain control of the situation.

4. Trust Your Instincts

Encounters with The Hugging Molly are often accompanied by an overwhelming sense of dread or a "sixth sense" that something is wrong. Trust this instinct. If you feel an inexplicable urge to leave an area, follow it. Your instincts are a primal survival tool, and listening to them may prevent you from wandering into her domain unknowingly.

5. Use Light as a Barrier

As she approaches, use your flashlight as a form of barrier, creating a line of light between you and her. Legends suggest that she is more reluctant to cross areas that are well-lit, and a strong light may be enough to delay her approach. Hold the flashlight steady and focus on breathing calmly, preparing to use your other tools if needed. Light symbolizes clarity and safety, reinforcing the boundaries between you and the spectral figure.

6. Have a Pre-Planned Escape Route

When traveling in areas known for sightings of The Hugging Molly, familiarize yourself with possible exit points and safe areas. Have a mental map of where you would go in the event of an encounter. This preparation not only provides an actual escape option but also instills confidence, knowing that you have an action plan in place.

Concluding Thoughts on Preparation

Preparing for an encounter with The Hugging Molly is as much about internal readiness as it is about physical preparation. By carrying essential items, cultivating mental resilience, and practicing calm, deliberate actions, you equip yourself to face the unknown with courage and control. An encounter with The Hugging Molly, should it occur, will test your composure and resolve, but with these preparations, you will be better equipped to emerge from the encounter unscathed.

In the next chapter, we will explore strategies for direct engagement, should avoidance prove impossible, offering practical techniques to manage her presence, communicate, and potentially defuse the encounter.

Chapter 5: Direct Engagement Strategies with The Hugging Molly

Despite your best efforts, there may come a time when avoiding The Hugging Molly becomes impossible. For those rare instances when she appears directly before you, it is crucial to be prepared with strategies for managing her presence, attempting communication, and defusing the encounter. While she is an unpredictable and otherworldly entity, reports from those who have survived direct engagements suggest that certain techniques may reduce her hostility or even prompt her to release her grip. This chapter provides a comprehensive guide for facing The Hugging Molly head-on, offering practical strategies that may help you manage her presence with resilience and control.

Managing Her Presence

The Hugging Molly's aura is overwhelming, her presence known to induce paralyzing fear, disorientation, and physical coldness. The first step in surviving an encounter is to stabilize your mental and emotional state to prevent panic. By managing her presence effectively, you can maintain control of your reactions, increasing your chances of emerging from the encounter unharmed.

1. Control Your Breathing

When faced with her, your body's natural response will be to enter a heightened state of fear. Combat this reaction by controlling your breathing, focusing on slow, deep breaths. A proven technique is the **4-7-8 breathing method**: inhale deeply for four seconds, hold your breath for seven seconds, and exhale slowly for eight seconds. This method activates the body's relaxation response, countering the surge of adrenaline and helping to keep your mind clear.

2. Maintain Eye Contact

The Hugging Molly's tendency to appear suddenly and silently can lead to a feeling of disorientation. If she appears within view, lock eyes with her as a way of asserting control over the encounter. Maintaining eye contact may help stabilize the situation, signaling both to her and to yourself that you are aware of her presence and unshaken by her sudden appearance. Eye contact can also help reduce the psychological sensation of vulnerability, giving you a foothold in the interaction.

3. Stand Your Ground

Resist the urge to back away or flee, as sudden movements may heighten her aggression or intensify her spectral approach. Stand your ground, keep your movements slow and deliberate, and avoid showing signs of fear, as her behavior may be influenced by the emotions she senses. By remaining rooted and calm, you communicate a message of respect and readiness, indicating that you will not succumb easily to panic or submission.

4. Acknowledge Her Presence

Although unconventional, acknowledging her presence in a calm and respectful tone has been noted by survivors as an effective strategy. Phrases such as "I see you" or "I know you are here" may affirm her existence in a way that reduces her perceived need to assert herself through fear. Acknowledgment shows that you recognize her presence without provoking her, potentially diffusing the intensity of the encounter.

Attempting Communication

The Hugging Molly's motives are mysterious, but some folklore suggests that she may be receptive to communication. If direct avoidance and basic management techniques are unsuccessful, attempting gentle, respectful communication may offer a means of placating her and possibly gaining insight into her intentions. While there is no guarantee that communication will yield positive results, it is worth trying as a last resort.

1. Use a Calm and Respectful Tone

If you choose to speak to her, do so in a calm and measured voice. Address her with respect, as though speaking to someone you wish to honor rather than fear. Refrain from asking demanding questions, as this may be interpreted as disrespectful. Instead, use statements or gentle inquiries, such as, "I am here in peace," or "What do you need?" This approach shows an openness to her intentions while avoiding any actions that could be perceived as confrontational.

2. Express Empathy or Understanding

Given that some legends attribute her behavior to unresolved grief, expressing empathy may resonate with her. Phrases like "I understand you may be hurting," or "I respect your loss," can communicate compassion, potentially softening her demeanor. This approach humanizes her presence, acknowledging her pain in a way that might encourage her to see you as an ally rather than an intruder.

3. Ask Permission to Leave

Some survivors have noted that politely asking for permission to leave may signal respect for her domain and reduce her hostility. Phrases like "I would like to leave in peace," or "May I go?" frame the encounter as one of mutual understanding rather than confrontation. This approach acknowledges her authority in the situation and may prompt her to grant you safe passage. The simple act of asking can create a symbolic boundary, showing that you are willing to respect her space if she allows it.

4. Speak in a Soothing, Repetitive Manner

If she shows signs of aggression, repeating a soothing phrase can help establish a calming rhythm in the interaction. Phrases like "It's all right" or "I mean no harm" spoken in a low, repetitive tone can create a rhythmic flow, which may help to dissipate the tension. This repetitive communication acts almost as a lullaby, potentially disrupting her intense focus and shifting the energy of the encounter.

Techniques to Defuse the Encounter

If the situation escalates to physical contact, such as The Hugging Molly's notorious hug, remaining calm and implementing specific defusion techniques may provide an opportunity to break free from her grip. While difficult, maintaining focus during this intense experience can make a critical difference in how the encounter unfolds.

1. Resist Struggling

Although your instinct will likely be to struggle or attempt to break free, such resistance is often counterproductive. The Hugging Molly's embrace is known to tighten in response to physical resistance. Instead, relax your body as much as possible, surrendering momentarily to her grip. This lack of struggle may reduce the intensity of her hold, as she may interpret calmness as a form of compliance or even respect. By relaxing, you signal a lack of threat, which may prompt her to lessen her grip.

2. Use Positive Visualization

If caught in her embrace, close your eyes and visualize a positive outcome, such as her releasing you and allowing you to leave safely. Imagine a warm, protective light surrounding you, creating a boundary between yourself and her presence. Visualizations like this have a grounding effect, allowing you to remain mentally strong and focused despite the overwhelming nature of the encounter. Some survivors claim that this visualization technique created a calming effect, reducing the severity of her grip and hastening the end of the encounter.

3. Recite Protective Words or Phrases

In moments of extreme fear, reciting a personal mantra, prayer, or affirmation can help to shield your mind and project an aura of protection. Phrases such as "I am safe," "I am protected," or a favorite line from a religious text can be empowering, fortifying your inner strength. This mental repetition can ground you, establishing a mental boundary that may encourage her to disengage. Additionally, focusing on these words can prevent your mind from spiraling into panic, providing an anchor in an otherwise overwhelming situation.

4. Invoke Symbols of Protection

Some cultures believe that invoking symbols of protection, either verbally or mentally, can deter spirits and negative entities. For instance, visualizing a protective symbol, such as a cross, pentacle, or other culturally significant image, may act as a shield. If you wear a symbol of protection, place your hand over it while envisioning it creating a barrier between you and The Hugging Molly. This invocation, even if symbolic, can reinforce your psychological defenses, fortifying your resolve and potentially weakening her grip.

5. Focus on Your Breathing and Centering Techniques

During her embrace, the fear of suffocation can be intense. To counter this sensation, focus on maintaining steady breaths, even if they are shallow. Mentally count each breath, allowing your mind to concentrate on a single point of focus. This technique can reduce panic, helping you avoid the physiological symptoms of fear, such as hyperventilation. Centering yourself during this moment of distress communicates mental strength, which may influence her perception of you as a calm, resilient individual.

6. Politely Request Release

As counterintuitive as it may seem, verbally requesting that she release you has reportedly worked for some individuals. Statements like "Please let me go" or "I would like to leave" voiced calmly may resonate with her, particularly if her intentions are rooted in sorrow rather than malice. By directly addressing her and asking for release, you assert your own agency in the encounter, showing her that you acknowledge her power but respectfully wish to exit the situation.

Summary and Final Thoughts on Direct Engagement

Facing The Hugging Molly is a daunting experience, one that challenges even the most resilient individuals. However, by remaining calm, managing her presence, and attempting respectful communication, you increase your chances of emerging from the encounter unscathed. Direct engagement requires careful balance: maintaining respect for her power while affirming your own intentions and presence. With these strategies, you can approach the situation with control, reducing the fear and vulnerability that she so often thrives upon.

While there is no guaranteed method for pacifying The Hugging Molly, these techniques provide a range of tools for confronting her presence. Should you ever find yourself face-to-face with this enigmatic figure, remember to stay grounded, trust in your preparations, and rely on the strategies outlined in this chapter.

Chapter 6: Geographic Hotspots of The Hugging Molly

The legend of The Hugging Molly is tied to specific geographic locations, regions, and paths that seem to attract her presence, and over time, these areas have become notorious hotspots for sightings. Understanding where these sightings occur can help both wary travelers and curious seekers either avoid her domain entirely or approach it with caution. In this chapter, we delve into the regions and places with frequent Hugging Molly encounters, offering maps and descriptions of these haunted areas, along with guidance on how to avoid or approach them safely.

Regions and Places with Frequent Sightings

The Hugging Molly is most commonly sighted in rural, isolated areas, often along lonely roads or in small towns with rich histories of folklore and supernatural legends. While her sightings are concentrated in specific hotspots, variations of her presence have been reported across the American South, particularly in Alabama, Texas, and other parts of the Deep South. Below are some of the most prominent areas where her sightings are most frequent.

1. Abbeville, Alabama

Abbeville, Alabama, is considered the birthplace of The Hugging Molly legend and remains the most well-documented hotspot for sightings. This small, historic town is known for its winding roads and quiet streets, which become eerily desolate after dark. Local lore holds that The Hugging Molly haunts the outskirts of the town, particularly near older sections and along paths leading into dense, wooded areas. Residents often warn visitors to avoid certain streets at night, particularly **Hickory Hollow Road** and **Creekside Trail**, where her presence is often felt.

- **Sightings Reported:** Many locals claim to have encountered The Hugging Molly while walking home in the evening, experiencing the classic symptoms of cold chills, footsteps behind them, and faint whispers. Those who have encountered her describe her towering figure appearing suddenly, often along abandoned roadsides.

- **Landmarks to Note:** Abandoned houses, narrow wooded paths, and an old railroad track are known markers near her territory.

2. Misty Valley, Texas

Misty Valley, Texas, is another area known for supernatural occurrences, including sightings of The Hugging Molly. This region is especially prone to dense fog rolling in during the evening, which locals believe provides her with an ideal cover. Misty Valley is notorious for its winding, forested roads and isolated trails, where travelers report unusual drops in temperature and shifting shadows that hint at her approach.

- **Sightings Reported:** Many witnesses describe hearing her scream echo through the valley, followed by cold mist enveloping the area. **Cedar Ridge Trail** and **Nightshade Pass** are particularly known for reported encounters, and visitors often recount feeling as though they are being watched from the shadows.
- **Landmarks to Note:** Cedar Ridge lookout and an old stone bridge are key markers where her presence has been reported.

3. Shadow Hollow, Louisiana

Shadow Hollow, a small community nestled in the swamplands of Louisiana, is reputed to be haunted by numerous spirits, including The Hugging Molly. The dark, winding roads surrounded by towering trees create an atmosphere ripe for sightings, and local legend holds that she is drawn to areas near water. Shadow Hollow has narrow paths and is lined with cypress trees that cast deep shadows, making her sudden appearance all the more disorienting.

- **Sightings Reported:** Encounters frequently occur near the **Blackwater Creek** and **Old Mill Road**, where people have described feeling the heavy weight of her grip and hearing whispers that seem to drift from the swamp itself. Nighttime fog and dense shadows often accompany these experiences.
- **Landmarks to Note:** Blackwater Creek crossing and an abandoned fishing cabin are specific locations where her presence has been recorded.

4. Haunted Pines of Willow Wood, Georgia

Willow Wood, Georgia, is home to an ancient forest known as the Haunted Pines, where The Hugging Molly is said to wander among the trees at night. The forest's twisted paths and dense canopy create an oppressive, shadowed atmosphere, and the silence is often described as unnervingly complete. Locals warn that her spirit is particularly active in late autumn, as fallen leaves blanket the forest floor and obscure the paths.

- **Sightings Reported:** Sightings here are usually accompanied by the sound of distant footsteps crunching on dry leaves. Witnesses recount feeling chills and spotting dark shapes among the trees, especially around **Raven's Path** and **Lost Oak Trail**.
- **Landmarks to Note:** The old Willow Wood Chapel and a small, overgrown cemetery are notable sites where her sightings are frequent.

5. Silent Woods of Raven's Peak, North Carolina

Raven's Peak is a secluded, mountainous area in North Carolina where The Hugging Molly has reportedly appeared to lone hikers and campers. The region's isolation, paired with the dense, silent woods, creates a chilling backdrop for encounters. Hikers often describe an eerie sense of being followed, as if unseen eyes are watching their every move.

- **Sightings Reported:** Witnesses in this area frequently experience sudden silence in the forest, hearing soft whispers or faint footsteps just behind them. Encounters are often reported along the **Old Mountain Trail** and **Cedar Hollow Path**, where people have felt her presence drawing close.
- **Landmarks to Note:** The abandoned Raven's Peak fire lookout and the nearby waterfall are known locations for sightings.

Maps and Descriptions of Known Haunted Areas

Each of these regions has distinct landmarks and paths that are associated with sightings of The Hugging Molly. Below is a brief map-based guide to navigating these areas, with recommendations for routes to avoid or explore cautiously:

1. **Abbeville, Alabama:** Focus on the eastern outskirts, particularly Hickory Hollow Road and Creekside Trail. Avoid these routes after dark, or approach with a flashlight and a strong sense of direction.
2. **Misty Valley, Texas:** The Cedar Ridge Trail and Nightshade Pass are prime locations for sightings. Travel in groups or avoid these areas altogether during evening hours.
3. **Shadow Hollow, Louisiana:** Blackwater Creek and Old Mill Road are frequent hotspots. Stick to main roads if traveling through this area and avoid side paths near the swamp.
4. **Willow Wood, Georgia:** Raven's Path and Lost Oak Trail wind through the Haunted Pines. Daytime visits are safe, but avoid these trails after sunset.
5. **Raven's Peak, North Carolina:** Old Mountain Trail and Cedar Hollow Path are isolated routes within Raven's Peak. If hiking, go in the company of others and carry a whistle or alarm.

How to Avoid These Zones (or Approach Them Safely)

For those who prefer to avoid The Hugging Molly's territory, the following guidelines can help you navigate around her hotspots. For the curious or courageous, safety measures are included for approaching these areas without compromising your well-being.

Avoiding Her Territory

1. **Stay on Main Roads and Well-Traveled Paths:** The Hugging Molly tends to appear in remote, isolated areas. Avoid taking unmarked trails or abandoned roads, as these are often where she is reported to emerge.
2. **Travel During Daylight Hours:** If you must travel near her hotspots, plan your route for daylight hours, as her appearances are exclusively tied to nighttime. Leave early to avoid being caught in her territory after dark.
3. **Avoid Foggy or Misty Conditions:** If the area is shrouded in mist, consider postponing your trip, as she is known to appear under foggy conditions that mask her approach.
4. **Stay in Groups:** The Hugging Molly is most often drawn to individuals who are alone. Traveling with a group reduces the likelihood of her singling you out and provides additional security in case of an unexpected encounter.

Approaching with Caution

For those who choose to enter her domain, approach with extreme care. The following precautions can help you explore these areas safely:

1. **Carry a High-Powered Flashlight and Spare Batteries:** A bright flashlight can help deter her approach, especially in dark, dense forests or foggy valleys. Keep spare batteries on hand to ensure your light source doesn't fail.

2. **Equip Yourself with a Personal Alarm or Whistle:** An alarm or whistle can create a loud noise that may startle or distract her. This sound can provide you with a chance to escape if you sense her approach.

3. **Establish a Check-In Routine:** Inform someone of your whereabouts and estimated return time before entering her hotspots. Set a check-in time and stick to it, so they can raise the alarm if you don't return as expected.

4. **Carry Protective Charms or Amulets:** As discussed in previous chapters, some people believe that carrying a personal charm or protective amulet can offer protection from supernatural entities. Choose a symbol or item with personal significance for added psychological comfort.

5. **Trust Your Instincts:** If you begin to feel uneasy, cold, or as though someone is watching you, trust your instincts and leave the area. Recognizing the warning signs is crucial, as lingering may increase the chances of an encounter.

6. **Be Aware of Environmental Cues:** Keep an eye out for common environmental indicators of her presence, such as sudden chills, unusual silence, or flickering lights. Awareness of these signs can give you the opportunity to exit before an encounter escalates.

Conclusion

Understanding the geographic hotspots of The Hugging Molly's sightings allows both cautious travelers and thrill-seekers to make informed choices. By knowing where her presence is most often reported, you can either avoid these areas entirely or approach them with respect and caution. Her legend is deeply rooted in specific places, each of which carries its own unique history and set of warnings. Whether you choose to steer clear of her domain or explore it with curiosity, preparation and awareness are essential.

In the next chapter, we will explore the folklore and cultural symbolism behind The Hugging Molly, examining how her legend reflects universal themes of fear, protection, and the unknown, and why her story endures across generations.

Chapter 7: Folklore and Cultural Symbolism of The Hugging Molly

The Hugging Molly's legend is more than just a tale of fear; it is a deeply embedded part of folklore that reflects universal themes of fear, protection, grief, and the unknown. Her story resonates across generations, transcending regional boundaries to become a symbol of both caution and mystery. In this chapter, we examine the folklore and cultural symbolism surrounding The Hugging Molly, exploring how her legend embodies shared human anxieties and societal values. We will uncover why her story endures, shedding light on the archetypes and themes she represents, and the cultural functions she serves.

The Folklore of Fear: Understanding The Hugging Molly as a Symbol of Dread

Fear is at the heart of The Hugging Molly's tale, making her a quintessential figure of nighttime terror. Her legend taps into our primal anxieties about the darkness and the dangers that lie within it. Like many supernatural figures, The Hugging Molly serves as a symbol of dread, an embodiment of the fears that we often repress or avoid confronting directly.

1. The Fear of the Unknown

The Hugging Molly's legend is steeped in mystery, and it is precisely her unknowability that amplifies the fear she instills. No one knows her true intentions or what compels her to embrace lone travelers. She exists in an ambiguous space, neither fully malicious nor benign, and this ambiguity heightens the unease surrounding her presence. This fear of the unknown is a universal human experience; the dark, the unseen, and the unexplained provoke a deep-seated anxiety that transcends cultural boundaries.

Her legend, like many ghostly tales, functions as a reminder of the limits of human knowledge and control. By embodying the unknown, she represents the aspects of life that remain beyond our understanding. This theme resonates across cultures, as each society grapples with the mysteries of existence and the boundaries of what can be known or explained. In this way, The Hugging Molly's story serves as a narrative space where people can explore and confront the unknown, making her a symbol of the fears we cannot fully explain.

2. The Fear of Isolation

Encounters with The Hugging Molly are often described as occurring in isolation, typically targeting individuals who are alone. This element of solitude reinforces the vulnerability that lies at the heart of her legend. Human beings are social creatures, and isolation can amplify feelings of insecurity, making us more susceptible to fear. By appearing only to those who are alone, The Hugging Molly's legend highlights a deep-seated fear of loneliness, a reminder of the psychological weight that solitude can carry.

In folklore, spirits and entities like The Hugging Molly often prey upon individuals who are alone or vulnerable, symbolizing the dangers associated with isolation. Her embrace, while terrifying, mirrors the desire for connection—albeit in a distorted, unsettling way. In this context, she can be seen as both a warning against wandering alone and a representation of the fear that solitude brings.

The Protector Archetype: The Hugging Molly as a Cautionary Guardian

Despite her fearsome reputation, some interpretations of The Hugging Molly's actions suggest that she operates as a distorted protector figure, driven by a desire to warn and guard rather than harm. This duality positions her within the archetype of the cautionary guardian, a common figure in folklore who uses fear to protect rather than destroy.

1. Fear as a Tool of Protection

Many legends depict her embrace not as an act of violence but as a means to prevent individuals from wandering alone in the dark, where real dangers might lie. Her presence serves as a deterrent, a cautionary figure who frightens people into staying safe. Similar figures appear across cultures, from "bogeyman" tales meant to keep children from wandering, to stories of forest spirits who guard against trespassers.

The Hugging Molly's embrace can be seen as a protective act, warning those who might otherwise come to harm. By creating fear, she encourages caution, embodying the message that the night is not always safe, and that vigilance is necessary. Her story functions as a form of social reinforcement, a reminder of the rules designed to keep people safe. This protective archetype underscores the idea that fear can serve as a powerful motivator, guiding behavior and instilling respect for the boundaries of the unknown.

2. Guardian of Tradition and Social Norms

The Hugging Molly's legend may also serve to reinforce social norms and traditional boundaries. In many cultures, spirits and supernatural figures act as guardians of customs, punishing those who stray from societal expectations or who venture into forbidden places. By embodying the consequences of wandering alone, The Hugging Molly's story supports traditional wisdom, urging people to heed community rules and respect safe practices.

Her legend reinforces the importance of adherence to these norms, particularly in rural or isolated communities where the dangers of the night are more immediate. Her story may have originated as a means to protect members of the community, especially the young, from the very real dangers of nocturnal travel. In this way, she serves a dual purpose: protecting individuals from physical danger while upholding societal values around safety and caution.

The Symbolism of Grief: The Hugging Molly as a Figure of Loss and Sorrow

Many variations of The Hugging Molly's story paint her as a figure driven by grief, a mother who lost her child and now roams the night seeking solace. This interpretation connects her to a broader theme of sorrow, positioning her as a symbol of unresolved loss and mourning. Her embrace, under this view, is not merely a tool of terror but an expression of yearning for connection.

1. The Archetype of the Mourning Mother

The figure of the grieving mother is a powerful archetype in folklore, appearing in legends around the world. These figures are often depicted as restless spirits, driven by an intense sorrow that binds them to the mortal world. The Hugging Molly's story aligns with this archetype, suggesting that her actions may be rooted in a need to alleviate her own loneliness or grief. Her embrace, while unsettling, is also a metaphor for the longing to reconnect with what she has lost.

In this context, The Hugging Molly's story reflects the universal experience of grief, a reminder of how loss can linger, shaping behavior and perception. Her legend provides a means for communities to acknowledge the power of sorrow and the way it can transform individuals, turning love and longing into actions that may appear frightening or irrational to outsiders.

2. Grief as a Driver of Haunting

The Hugging Molly's legend suggests that she is trapped in a cycle of grief, unable to find peace until she reconnects with what she has lost. This theme resonates with cultural beliefs about the dead and the concept of unfinished business. In folklore, spirits often remain earthbound due to unresolved emotions or incomplete tasks. The Hugging Molly's story suggests that her nightly wanderings are a form of haunting rooted in emotional attachment, emphasizing the impact of unprocessed grief.

Through her story, communities can explore the enduring nature of grief and the ways it can shape one's actions. Her legend provides a safe space for individuals to confront and acknowledge the weight of loss, allowing society to integrate the reality of sorrow into a shared narrative. This function of her story is especially relevant in communities where the dead are honored and remembered, as it reinforces the idea that the bonds between the living and the departed endure beyond death.

The Hugging Molly as a Bridge Between the Living and the Supernatural

The Hugging Molly occupies a liminal space, existing between the realms of the living and the supernatural. Her story reflects humanity's fascination with what lies beyond, tapping into our collective curiosity and fear of what happens after death. By embodying this bridge, she serves as a reminder of the thin veil that separates life and death, inviting us to confront the mysteries that lie just beyond our understanding.

1. A Messenger from the Other Side

In some interpretations, The Hugging Molly's presence serves as a reminder of the supernatural realm and its proximity to our own. Her appearances at night, when the boundaries between worlds are believed to be thinnest, position her as a messenger from the other side. She exists as a symbol of mortality, an eerie reminder that death is ever-present and that the spirit world is not as distant as we might like to believe.

Her story fulfills a psychological need to engage with the idea of an afterlife, providing a narrative space for communities to explore the possibilities of what happens beyond death. This function serves to reinforce cultural beliefs about the supernatural and offers a means of addressing existential questions through folklore, allowing individuals to confront the unknown in a way that is indirect yet meaningful.

2. The Veil Between Life and Death

The Hugging Molly's legend aligns with cultural beliefs about liminal spaces, such as crossroads, thresholds, and nighttime, where the boundary between life and death is believed to blur. By appearing at night and in isolated places, she becomes a figure of transition, representing the unknown that lies on the other side of the veil. Her embrace, which feels both protective and constricting, mirrors the tension between life and death, evoking both fear and fascination.

This symbolism positions her as a guide of sorts, albeit one who is shrouded in darkness and mystery. Her story suggests that while death may be inevitable, the journey between realms is one that requires respect and caution. In this way, her legend serves as a cultural reminder of the thin line that separates our world from the unknown, a theme that has captured human imagination for centuries.

Why The Hugging Molly's Story Endures

The Hugging Molly's legend endures because it taps into universal themes that resonate across cultures and generations. Her story addresses fundamental human fears, societal values, and existential questions, providing a space for individuals to explore and process these themes within a narrative framework. By embodying the unknown, the protective, and the sorrowful, she becomes a multifaceted symbol, one that continues to captivate and haunt the imagination.

Her story also endures because it offers a sense of continuity, linking the present with the past through shared folklore. Legends like hers connect people to their heritage, preserving cultural values and communal wisdom. As long as there is a need to confront fear, respect tradition, and ponder the mysteries of existence, The Hugging Molly's legend will continue to hold a place in the collective consciousness, serving as both a cautionary tale and a source of fascination.

Chapter 8: Understanding the Rules of Engagement with The Hugging Molly

Encounters with The Hugging Molly can be deeply unsettling, but understanding the "rules of engagement" can help you approach these experiences with greater confidence and control. Like many supernatural entities in folklore, she appears to respond to specific actions, behaviors, and attitudes, and respecting these unspoken rules may increase your chances of surviving a direct encounter unscathed. In this chapter, we will cover the essential do's and don'ts during an encounter, key behavioral tips to minimize risk, and cultural superstitions surrounding interactions with spirits like The Hugging Molly. By following these guidelines, you can approach her with caution and respect, enhancing your chances of a safe outcome.

Do's and Don'ts During an Encounter

Knowing what to do—and what to avoid—can make a significant difference when facing The Hugging Molly. Observing these guidelines can help you navigate the encounter without unintentionally provoking her or increasing the risk of harm.

Do's

1. **Remain Calm and Composed**
   - Maintaining composure is one of the most important actions you can take during an encounter. Fear and panic may draw her closer, as she is believed to be drawn to heightened emotional states. Deep breathing, steadying your thoughts, and keeping your body relaxed can all communicate calmness and control, reducing the likelihood of escalating the encounter.

2. **Acknowledge Her Presence**
   - Acknowledging her respectfully can signal that you are aware of her authority in the situation. Phrases such as "I see you" or "I acknowledge you" may show that you recognize her existence without defying her presence. This ac-

knowledgment can serve as a subtle form of respect, often helping to keep the encounter peaceful.

3. **Speak Softly and Respectfully**
   - If you choose to speak, use a soft, respectful tone. Loud voices or demands may be interpreted as challenges, which can provoke a negative reaction. Phrases like "I mean no harm" or "I respect your space" indicate that you come without ill intent, which may encourage her to act less aggressively.

4. **Move Slowly and Deliberately**
   - Avoid sudden or jerky movements, which can trigger a defensive reaction. Slow, deliberate motions signal calmness and control, helping to reduce her perceived need to act as a threat. If you need to turn or step back, do so in a controlled manner, maintaining your composure.

5. **Hold a Protective Object with Intent**
   - Holding a protective amulet or charm can help bolster your confidence, which may influence the energy of the encounter. These objects carry psychological significance and may provide a sense of security that helps you stay grounded. Some believe that certain symbols can serve as a boundary between you and supernatural forces, offering a subtle form of protection.

6. **Use a Gentle Gesture of Peace**
   - Some witnesses recommend extending an open palm or offering a gentle nod as a symbol of peace. This nonverbal cue shows that you approach with a willingness to respect her domain, acknowledging her presence without appearing confrontational.

Don'ts

1. Avoid Staring Aggressively

- Although it's advisable to maintain awareness of her, aggressive eye contact can be perceived as a challenge. Avoid intense or direct staring, which may signal defiance. Instead, keep her in view without locking your gaze aggressively, as this shows you're aware but not confrontational.

2. Do Not Shout or Make Loud Noises

- Loud noises may be seen as acts of disrespect or attempts to overpower her, which can provoke her anger. This includes yelling, clapping, or sudden outbursts, as they may disrupt the delicate balance of the encounter. Instead, keep your tone and volume subdued to avoid startling or provoking her.

3. Refrain from Physical Touch

- Physical contact, even if unintentional, is generally discouraged in encounters with spirits. Attempting to touch her may escalate the encounter or increase her hold on you. If you feel her presence drawing closer, resist the urge to reach out, as folklore suggests that breaking the boundary between you could intensify her grip.

4. Don't Turn Your Back Completely

- Although fleeing is not advised, turning your back on her entirely can be perceived as disrespect or dismissal. Instead, if you choose to leave, do so slowly and sideways, showing awareness of her presence while avoiding direct confrontation.

5. Avoid Challenging or Mocking Her

- Spirits like The Hugging Molly are believed to be sensitive to disrespect, and taunting or challenging her can have severe consequences. Avoid any words or gestures that could be interpreted as mockery, as her response to disrespect can be swift and intense.

6. **Don't Ignore Warning Signs**
   ◦ If you begin to feel chills, hear whispers, or notice a sudden drop in temperature, take these signs seriously. Ignoring these early warnings can increase your chances of a full encounter. Acknowledging these signs and preparing yourself may help reduce her intensity and keep the situation under control.

Key Behavioral Tips to Minimize Risk

Certain behaviors and attitudes are known to help minimize risk in encounters with supernatural beings like The Hugging Molly. By maintaining respectful boundaries and following these best practices, you increase your chances of a safer experience.

1. Adopt a Mindset of Respect

Respect is crucial when dealing with spirits. Approach the encounter as you would a meeting with an elder or someone of authority. Treat her presence as sacred or mysterious, and avoid trivializing the experience. This mindset of respect can help you act with caution, honoring her presence rather than provoking it.

2. Remain Grounded and Confident

Standing your ground and exuding calm confidence can be effective in encounters with The Hugging Molly. Spirits are believed to sense energy, and projecting stability and self-assurance may signal that you are not easily swayed by fear. This grounded confidence establishes a boundary of mental resilience, reducing her influence over you.

3. Demonstrate Humility and Openness

Humility is valued in encounters with spirits, as it indicates a willingness to accept the unknown without presuming superiority. Showing openness to her presence, without challenging or doubting it, may create a neutral energy that keeps the encounter balanced. This humility acknowledges her role without presuming to understand or control it.

4. Use Protective Mantras or Prayers

In many cultures, protective mantras, prayers, or affirmations are used to create a sense of psychological and spiritual safety. Reciting a familiar verse, affirmation, or prayer can bolster your resolve and shield your mind against fear. These words serve as an anchor, focusing your thoughts and building an internal boundary that may ward off negative influences.

5. Show Awareness Without Engaging Emotionally

Acknowledging her presence without succumbing to heightened emotions like fear or curiosity is another effective approach. By observing her calmly, you create an emotional distance that can keep you from being "drawn in" by her energy. This balance of awareness without engagement allows you to maintain control, reducing the risk of a prolonged or intense encounter.

6. Trust Your Intuition and Respect Your Limits

If at any point you feel an instinctive urge to leave, trust this feeling. Many cultures believe that intuition is heightened in supernatural encounters and that ignoring it can lead to negative consequences. Respect your own boundaries and limits, as doing so can reinforce your sense of agency and prevent you from overstaying in her presence.

Cultural Superstitions Around Dealing with Spirits

Cultural traditions worldwide offer insights into dealing with spirits and supernatural entities, reflecting beliefs and practices that have been passed down for generations. These superstitions provide valuable guidance on how to engage respectfully, drawing on centuries of wisdom regarding the proper ways to interact with beings from the beyond.

1. The Use of Salt as a Barrier

In many cultures, salt is believed to act as a barrier against spirits and negative entities. Carrying a small vial of salt or creating a circle of salt around you is thought to provide protection from supernatural harm. If you feel The Hugging Molly's presence drawing close, sprinkling salt in a circle around yourself may offer a psychological or spiritual shield, creating a boundary that could help contain her approach.

2. Avoiding Mention of Names During Encounters

In various traditions, speaking the names of spirits during an encounter is discouraged, as it may strengthen their presence or draw them closer. Refrain from referring to The Hugging Molly directly by name during an encounter, as this act of naming can be seen as an invitation. Instead, use neutral language, like "the presence" or "the spirit," to avoid personalizing the interaction.

3. Offering Coins or Gifts as a Gesture of Respect

Some cultures believe that offering small tokens, like coins, can serve as a sign of respect, appeasing spirits and keeping them from harm. Carrying a few coins, dried herbs, or other symbolic tokens may allow you to create a peace offering, signaling to The Hugging Molly that you approach with honor and humility. These offerings may act as a form of goodwill, reducing the chances of a negative encounter.

4. The Power of Iron and Cold Steel

In many European traditions, cold iron or steel is believed to repel supernatural beings, as these materials are thought to possess grounding properties. Carrying a small iron object, such as a nail or key, may provide protection, symbolically grounding your presence and reinforcing your boundary. If you feel her presence intensifying, holding an iron object may bolster your confidence and help deflect negative energy.

5. Using Sage or Protective Herbs for Cleansing

Herbs like sage, lavender, and rosemary are often used in spiritual practices to cleanse spaces and create protective energy. Carrying a small bundle of dried herbs or a sprig of rosemary can act as a personal amulet, creating an aura of protection. While burning sage may not be feasible during an encounter, simply carrying these herbs can have a grounding effect, offering a subtle layer of safety.

6. Avoiding Eye Contact with the Dead

In certain cultural beliefs, making direct eye contact with spirits can establish a link that prolongs the encounter or invites them closer. To avoid intensifying her presence, consider keeping your gaze slightly averted, focusing on peripheral awareness rather than direct eye contact. This practice respects the boundary between worlds, symbolizing a subtle form of acknowledgment without full engagement.

Concluding Thoughts on the Rules of Engagement

Navigating an encounter with The Hugging Molly requires knowledge, respect, and a calm presence of mind. By following these rules of engagement, you acknowledge her domain and power, allowing for a balanced interaction that reduces the chances of an escalated experience. These guidelines, rooted in both behavioral principles and cultural superstitions, provide a framework for approaching her with care, empowering you to face the unknown with resilience.

Chapter 9: Escaping the Embrace of The Hugging Molly

An encounter with The Hugging Molly can quickly escalate from an eerie presence to a physical embrace—a constricting hug that has left many feeling shaken and disoriented. This embrace, while not deadly, is known for its intensity, often leaving victims immobilized and overwhelmed. In this chapter, we explore tactics to use if she approaches and initiates an embrace, covering physical, mental, and emotional strategies to help you stay safe. Additionally, we'll discuss common mistakes to avoid during such encounters, as they can lead to more severe and prolonged experiences.

Tactics to Use if Approached

If you sense that The Hugging Molly is drawing near, specific tactics can help you prepare for her approach and potentially avoid the embrace altogether. Remaining aware of these strategies can be crucial, especially when early signs like footsteps, chills, or whispers indicate that she is closing in.

1. Identify an Exit Route

When you first sense her presence, scan your surroundings and mentally map out a potential exit. Identify clear paths, routes back to populated areas, or places with light. Knowing an exit in advance allows you to move quickly and confidently if she begins to close the distance. Avoid turning your back completely, but gradually shift yourself in the direction of the chosen exit, ready to leave if the encounter escalates.

2. Create Physical Boundaries

If you have items like a flashlight, personal alarm, or even a protective amulet, use them to create a physical boundary. Shine a bright light in her direction, which folklore suggests can deter spirits who thrive in darkness. Activate your personal alarm to startle her, or hold your protective amulet close to your chest as a symbolic shield. These boundaries serve as mental barriers as well, reminding you of the control you have in the situation.

3. Control Your Body Language

Adopting calm, controlled body language can reduce the intensity of her approach. Standing tall and relaxed, with a slightly open stance, signals resilience and a lack of fear. Avoid defensive postures like crossing your arms or clenching fists, as these may signal nervousness or aggression. Projecting calm through your body language can reduce her need to assert herself physically, helping you to maintain a sense of control.

4. Acknowledge Her Presence Verbally

Softly acknowledging her presence with a respectful phrase, like "I see you" or "I know you're here," may appease her and prevent her from closing in. Many believe that spirits respond to respectful recognition, which could help maintain a comfortable distance. By speaking calmly, you communicate that you are aware of her without challenging her authority or attempting to ignore her presence.

Physical, Mental, and Emotional Tactics to Stay Safe

If The Hugging Molly initiates the embrace, your ability to respond with calm and controlled actions can make a significant difference. The following physical, mental, and emotional strategies can help you endure and potentially break free from her grip.

Physical Tactics

1. Relax Your Body

Though it may seem counterintuitive, relaxing your body is one of the most effective ways to reduce the intensity of her grip. Tension or physical resistance tends to heighten her hold, as her embrace tightens in response to physical struggle. By relaxing, you signal nonresistance, which may weaken her grip or prevent it from intensifying. Focus on loosening each muscle group, allowing your body to remain as fluid and relaxed as possible.

2.Slow, Shallow Breaths

The Hugging Molly's embrace often restricts breathing, which can quickly lead to panic. To counter this, practice shallow, controlled breaths. Inhale slowly and exhale deliberately, focusing on each breath to prevent hyperventilation. This controlled breathing helps you conserve energy and reduce physical discomfort, maintaining a sense of calm despite the constraint.

3.Hold a Protective Object Firmly

If you are holding a protective charm or object, grip it firmly and hold it close to your body. Many believe that certain objects, especially those with personal significance, can help maintain a boundary between yourself and supernatural entities. The act of holding something tangi-

ble also provides grounding, which can reduce panic and keep you focused.

4.Move Your Fingers or Toes

When immobilized, subtle physical movements like wiggling your
fingers or toes can help maintain control over your body. These small
movements reinforce your autonomy and prevent feelings of helplessness. By keeping some part of your body active, you maintain a sense of
agency, which can reduce the psychological impact of her embrace.

Mental Tactics

1. Focus on a Mental Anchor

Choose a comforting phrase, image, or memory as a mental anchor, and focus on it to distract your mind from fear. Some survivors of encounters with The Hugging Molly report that reciting a mantra like "I am safe" or visualizing a protective light surrounding them helped them endure the embrace. This mental anchor serves as a psychological shield, keeping you centered and reducing the power of her influence.

2. Use Visualization Techniques

Imagine a protective barrier or bright light surrounding you, creating a boundary between yourself and her presence. This visualization can reinforce a sense of safety, as though you are shielded by an invisible force. Picture this light or barrier expanding outward, symbolically pushing her away. Visualization empowers you to maintain control over your mental space, even in a situation that feels physically restrictive.

3. Count Your Breaths

Counting breaths is a simple but effective way to stay focused and prevent your mind from spiraling into fear. By counting each inhale and exhale, you maintain a rhythm that stabilizes your thoughts and prevents panic from taking hold. This mental exercise also keeps your focus inward, providing a buffer against the unsettling external environment.

4.Engage in Mindful Observation

Mentally observe each sensation without reacting to it. Note the pressure of her grip, the sound of her breathing, or the feeling of coldness, but resist the urge to assign judgment or panic. By simply observing these sensations, you create an emotional distance that helps reduce fear. This mindful approach can diminish the impact of the encounter, allowing you to endure it with a level of detachment.

Emotional Tactics

1. Acknowledge and Accept Fear

Acknowledging fear, rather than suppressing it, can help you remain emotionally grounded. Accepting that you feel afraid without allowing it to control you creates emotional resilience. This acknowledgment reduces the fear's power, allowing you to confront it rationally rather than emotionally. Repeat to yourself, "I feel fear, and that's okay. I am still in control."

2.Cultivate Compassion for Her Presence

Some believe that The Hugging Molly's actions are rooted in unresolved sorrow or grief. By cultivating compassion, you can view her embrace as an expression of her own suffering rather than an attack. Recognizing her as a figure of sorrow can help reduce fear, transforming the encounter from one of terror to one of understanding. This shift in perspective can make the experience feel less threatening.

3.Remain Emotionally Neutral

If compassion is difficult to access, aim for emotional neutrality. Imagine yourself as a passive observer, neither attached nor repulsed by her presence. This neutrality creates a buffer that minimizes the intensity of the encounter, allowing you to experience it without deep emotional investment. Emotional neutrality reduces the psychological toll, allowing you to retain clarity and composure.

4.Channel Resilience with Self-Statements

Reinforce your resilience by repeating self-statements like "I am strong" or "I can endure this." These affirmations act as mental armor, reminding you of your inner strength. By focusing on resilience, you create an emotional boundary that can mitigate the impact of her embrace and help you stay grounded.

Common Mistakes to Avoid

Avoiding certain actions and reactions can make a critical difference in the outcome of the encounter. The following are common mistakes that can exacerbate her embrace or lead to a more intense experience.

1. Panicking or Struggling

Panic and physical struggle often heighten The Hugging Molly's grip, as these reactions may provoke her need to assert control. Avoid thrashing, screaming, or making erratic movements, as these can worsen the situation. Instead, focus on calming your breathing and relaxing your muscles, as these actions signal nonresistance.

2. Engaging in Confrontational Behavior

Confrontational behavior, such as yelling or attempting to push her away, can be interpreted as a challenge. This behavior often escalates her response, leading to a tighter embrace or a more intense experience. Refrain from any form of aggression or resistance, as her reaction to defiance is known to be swift and severe.

3. Failing to Recognize Early Signs

Ignoring early warning signs, such as chills, whispers, or shifting shadows, can lead to an unprepared encounter. These signs are subtle cues that allow you to mentally and physically prepare before she initiates contact. Recognizing and acknowledging these signs can provide valuable seconds to ready yourself.

4. Allowing Fear to Take Control

Fear is natural, but allowing it to control your actions can intensify her grip. When fear spirals unchecked, it can lead to panic, making it difficult to focus on tactics or maintain composure. Acknowledge your fear without letting it overwhelm you, using breathing and visualization techniques to manage it constructively.

5. Over-Fixating on the Encounter

While in her embrace, some people become hyper-focused on the experience itself, which can amplify sensations of fear and helplessness. Instead, redirect your attention to calming thoughts or mantras, allowing your mind to "soften" the encounter by shifting focus. Over-fixating can intensify feelings of vulnerability, whereas redirecting your thoughts can help maintain a sense of distance.

Concluding Thoughts on Escaping the Embrace

Escaping The Hugging Molly's embrace requires a balanced approach of physical relaxation, mental focus, and emotional resilience. By remaining calm, avoiding common mistakes, and employing these strategies, you can increase your chances of enduring her grip without succumbing to panic or helplessness. While her embrace is daunting, preparation and self-assurance can significantly influence the encounter's outcome.

Chapter 10: Self-Defense Strategies Against The Hugging Molly

Though The Hugging Molly is a supernatural entity, there are physical, mental, and spiritual self-defense strategies that may help you withstand or even repel her presence. The key to protecting yourself lies in a combination of effective movements, self-protection tools and charms, and techniques to maintain composure under pressure. This chapter will guide you through these methods, equipping you with practical skills and items that can make a significant difference when facing The Hugging Molly or similar supernatural threats.

Effective Movements and Techniques

Even though The Hugging Molly's embrace is supernatural in nature, certain body movements and physical techniques can help you avoid her grip or lessen its intensity. While traditional self-defense tactics may not apply in full, adapting these principles can give you an edge during an encounter.

1. Circular Movements and Defensive Pivots

If you sense her approaching, try to avoid direct, linear movements, as turning away from her too quickly can provoke her or escalate the encounter. Instead, practice small, circular pivots or side steps. Circular movements allow you to keep her within your peripheral vision without fully turning your back. Maintaining this angled stance reduces vulnerability and keeps your balance centered, providing a sense of stability and control.

2. Protective Arm Positioning

When facing her approach, position your arms in front of you in a loose, open stance, as though holding an invisible barrier between you and her. Avoid crossing your arms or holding them tightly, as these defensive postures can signal fear. This open positioning establishes a physical boundary while keeping you ready to deflect her grip if she draws close. If she reaches out, you can use a gentle push with your palms to create a small amount of space between you, without signaling aggression.

3. Grounding Stance with Low Center of Gravity

To maintain stability, assume a grounded stance by bending your knees slightly and centering your weight over your feet. This posture keeps you balanced, making it harder for her to pull you off-center. It also helps you stay anchored, which can prevent you from feeling overwhelmed by her presence. In situations where her grip tightens, a grounded stance enhances your physical resilience, helping you withstand the pressure.

4. Controlled Backward Steps

If her approach is persistent, taking small, controlled steps backward can give you space without signaling panic. As you move, focus on maintaining a steady rhythm, avoiding sudden or erratic movements. Slow steps reinforce calmness, showing that you are in control of the encounter. Controlled backward movement also allows you to slowly increase the distance without breaking eye contact, which can reduce the likelihood of a sudden escalation.

5. Use of Defensive Blocks

If her arms extend toward you, you may instinctively raise your forearms in a defensive block. While her grip is notoriously strong, using your forearms to create a barrier can lessen the direct impact of her initial touch. Cross your forearms loosely in front of your chest, creating a small buffer zone. This position can help absorb the pressure of her grip, providing a slight psychological advantage and giving you a moment to regain composure.

Tools and Charms for Self-Protection

Folklore and cultural traditions offer various tools, charms, and symbols believed to repel spirits or reduce their influence. While these items may not guarantee full protection, they can provide a valuable layer of defense, both psychologically and energetically, during an encounter with The Hugging Molly.

1. Protective Charms or Amulets

Many cultures use protective charms or amulets to ward off supernatural entities. Consider carrying a small charm that holds personal significance, such as a cross, an evil eye pendant, or a protective rune. These symbols act as psychological anchors, helping you feel grounded and shielded. If she approaches, hold the charm tightly and visualize it creating a protective barrier around you.

- **Example Charms:** Cross, hamsa, pentacle, or a piece of obsidian. Each of these is traditionally associated with repelling negative energy and protecting against harmful entities.

2. Salt

Salt has long been used in various cultures as a protective agent against spirits. If possible, carry a small vial of salt with you, and if you sense her drawing close, sprinkle a line of salt between you and her as a symbolic boundary. Alternatively, placing a small circle of salt around yourself can act as a spiritual shield, creating a psychological and physical barrier that may deter her from stepping closer.

3. Iron or Cold Steel

Many folklore traditions believe that iron repels spirits, grounding supernatural energy. Carrying a small iron item, such as an iron nail, key, or horseshoe charm, may help shield you. If you feel her approach, hold the iron object firmly as a grounding point, visualizing it as a powerful source of protection. Some survivors of supernatural encounters report that the presence of iron seemed to lessen the intensity of the entity's approach.

4. Mirror or Reflective Object

Mirrors are often thought to deflect or confuse spirits, reflecting their energy back upon themselves. Carrying a small mirror or compact may offer a unique defense; if she approaches, hold the mirror facing outward as if to reflect her image back. Folklore suggests that spirits are sometimes unsettled by their own reflection, and while not a guaranteed deterrent, it may provide a momentary disruption in her approach.

5. Sage or Protective Herbs

Herbs such as sage, rosemary, and lavender are traditionally associated with cleansing and protection. Carrying a small bundle of dried sage or a sprig of rosemary can serve as a protective amulet. If you sense her presence, hold the herb close to your chest and visualize it as a cleansing force that surrounds you. In the aftermath of an encounter, sage or rosemary can be used to cleanse any residual energy, restoring a sense of calm.

6. Personal Alarm or Whistle

While not supernatural, a personal alarm or whistle can disrupt her approach, creating a loud noise that may startle her or shift the energy of the encounter. In moments of high intensity, activate the alarm or blow the whistle to create a break in the silence, which may give you a brief opportunity to create distance. The sudden noise serves as both a physical and psychological disruption, allowing you to regain control.

How to Maintain Composure Under Pressure

Encounters with The Hugging Molly can be terrifying, making it essential to cultivate techniques that help maintain composure. The following strategies will help you regulate fear, focus on rational thoughts, and prevent panic from taking hold.

1. Deep Breathing Techniques

Controlled breathing is one of the most effective tools for staying calm. Practice deep breathing methods, such as the 4-4-4 technique (inhale for four seconds, hold for four seconds, exhale for four seconds), to maintain a steady breath and slow your heart rate. Breathing techniques engage the parasympathetic nervous system, reducing the body's stress response and helping you regain mental clarity.

2. Grounding Visualization

Use grounding visualizations to connect with the physical world around you. Imagine roots extending from your feet into the earth, anchoring you securely. This grounding technique reinforces a sense of physical and mental stability, counteracting the feeling of being overwhelmed by her supernatural presence. Visualizing this connection to the earth can provide a sense of empowerment, helping you stay focused.

3. Mental Anchors and Mantras

Choose a personal mantra or mental anchor, such as "I am safe" or "I am in control," and repeat it silently to maintain focus. A mental anchor prevents the mind from wandering into fearful or irrational thoughts, grounding you in a reassuring phrase. This simple practice can make a significant difference in maintaining composure, as it reinforces inner strength and mental clarity.

4. Centering Exercises

Centering exercises are useful for maintaining balance and focus in high-stress situations. Place your hand over your chest or on a protective charm, focusing on the sensation of physical contact. This grounding gesture can help you reconnect with your body, keeping you present in the moment and preventing your mind from spiraling into panic.

5. Focusing on Your Senses

Engage your senses to bring yourself back to the present. Note the feeling of the ground beneath you, the sounds around you, or the sensation of cool air. Focusing on sensory details keeps you aware of your surroundings without allowing fear to dominate. This sensory awareness creates a layer of mental resilience, reminding you that you are grounded in the physical world, even in the face of a supernatural presence.

6. Channeling Confidence and Resilience

Remind yourself of past moments when you faced fear and prevailed. Drawing on memories of resilience reinforces self-belief, allowing you to channel confidence even under pressure. By remembering past successes in overcoming fear, you build a psychological foundation that helps you face the encounter with a calm, composed attitude.

Common Mistakes to Avoid During Self-Defense

During high-stress situations like an encounter with The Hugging Molly, certain actions can inadvertently escalate the situation or weaken your defenses. Avoiding these mistakes can help you maintain a stronger boundary and increase the effectiveness of your self-defense strategies.

1. Panicking or Freezing Up

Fear can trigger a "fight or flight" response that may lead to panic or freezing up. Freezing can make you feel trapped, intensifying feelings of helplessness. Instead, focus on calming breaths and visualizations to keep your mind active and prevent complete immobilization.

2. Excessive Physical Struggle

Physical struggle against supernatural entities like The Hugging Molly is often ineffective and can increase her hold. Struggling not only wastes energy but can also heighten the intensity of her grip. Instead, practice grounding and relaxation techniques, which help reduce her influence and allow for a less intense encounter.

3. Ignoring Protective Tools

Forgetting to use protective tools and charms can weaken your defenses. In high-stress encounters, it's easy to overlook the items you've prepared, so practice holding and visualizing their purpose in advance. Keeping these tools in a designated pocket or accessible location allows you to deploy them without hesitation.

4. Losing Focus on Your Breathing

Rapid breathing and hyperventilation exacerbate feelings of fear and helplessness. If you notice your breathing becoming erratic, redirect your focus to deep, slow breaths to maintain a sense of control and prevent panic from overtaking your mind.

5. Allowing Fear to Control Your Mindset

Fear can distort perception and amplify sensations of vulnerability. If you feel fear creeping in, acknowledge it without letting it control you. Refocus on grounding techniques and remind yourself that you are equipped to handle the encounter. This balance of awareness and resilience reinforces a mental boundary that can help you endure her presence.

Concluding Thoughts on Self-Defense Strategies

Facing The Hugging Molly requires preparation, resilience, and a calm approach. By employing effective movements, carrying protective tools, and maintaining composure under pressure, you can strengthen your defenses and navigate the encounter with control and confidence. The strategies outlined in this chapter equip you with a range of options for self-protection, blending physical, mental, and spiritual techniques to help you withstand even the most intense encounters with supernatural forces.

Chapter 11: Equipment for Protection Against The Hugging Molly

When facing supernatural entities like The Hugging Molly, having the right equipment for protection can make a critical difference. From traditional talismans and herbs to modern gadgets, each item serves as a layer of defense, helping to bolster your mental resilience, shield against unwanted advances, and provide early warning signals. This chapter will guide you through recommended protective gear and supplies, covering traditional tools rooted in folklore, natural elements believed to repel spirits, and contemporary technology that may offer an advantage during an encounter.

Recommended Gear and Supplies

Preparing for an encounter requires a combination of practical, spiritual, and psychological tools. These recommended items can serve as your primary defenses, helping to create boundaries, maintain awareness, and offer a sense of security in situations where The Hugging Molly's presence is felt.

1. Flashlight (High-Lumen)

A powerful flashlight is one of the most essential items to carry, as spirits like The Hugging Molly are often associated with darkness. A high-lumen flashlight can pierce through fog and shadows, creating a physical and symbolic boundary. Choose a flashlight with at least 500 lumens to ensure strong illumination, and carry spare batteries to avoid being left in the dark. Many believe that bright light disrupts supernatural entities, so using a flashlight may deter her from closing in.

2. Personal Alarm or Whistle

A personal alarm or whistle creates a sudden, loud noise that can startle and disrupt her approach. In folklore, noise is often used to scare away spirits, as it creates an intense shift in energy. These items serve both as a deterrent and a psychological shield, giving you a sense of control during a high-stress moment. The sound may also alert others nearby, offering a layer of social protection if you are within earshot of assistance.

3. Protective Clothing

Consider wearing long sleeves and sturdy clothing to add a physical barrier between yourself and her touch. While this may not provide direct protection against her grip, having an extra layer can offer psychological comfort and act as a subtle form of resistance. Choose fabrics that make you feel grounded and secure, such as cotton or wool, to enhance your mental and physical resilience.

4. Mirror or Reflective Object

A small handheld mirror or reflective item can serve as a defense tool by symbolically reflecting her energy back upon herself. Many traditions believe that spirits are unsettled by their own reflection, as it forces them to confront their spectral nature. In an encounter, hold the mirror outward and avoid looking directly into it, as this action may increase the strength of the reflection. A mirror compact or polished metal surface, like a locket, can be discreet yet effective.

5. Salt (Small Container or Sachet)

Salt is one of the most widely used protective items in folklore, believed to create a boundary that spirits cannot cross. Carry a small vial or sachet of salt, and if you feel her presence drawing close, sprinkle a line of salt around yourself or create a small circle. This action symbolizes a protective barrier and serves as a mental anchor, reinforcing your boundary and increasing your confidence. Alternatively, holding the salt container tightly can help you feel grounded.

6. First Aid Kit

While a first aid kit may not directly protect you from The Hugging Molly, it is essential to be prepared in case of physical or emotional shock. Items such as antiseptic wipes, bandages, and calming ointments (e.g., lavender balm) can provide comfort if you experience scratches, bruises, or heightened anxiety. This practical kit can help bring you back to the physical realm and assist in post-encounter recovery.

Traditional Talismans, Herbs, and Symbols Believed to Repel Spirits

In many cultures, certain symbols, herbs, and objects are believed to repel spirits and create protective energy. These traditional items, often rooted in folklore, can provide a psychological advantage and help create boundaries between you and supernatural forces.

1. Iron Objects

Iron has long been regarded as a protective material, believed to repel spirits and ground energy. Consider carrying a small iron object, such as a nail, key, or horseshoe charm, as a defense against The Hugging Molly. Holding iron can help reduce fear, as its weight and coldness provide a tangible connection to the physical world, creating a barrier against supernatural influence.

- **Best Iron Items for Protection:** Iron nail, small horseshoe, or iron ring. These items are easy to carry and can be gripped tightly during an encounter.

2. Amulets with Protective Symbols

Amulets featuring protective symbols, such as crosses, hamsas, pentacles, or the evil eye, are often worn to shield against harmful entities. Each symbol carries a unique cultural significance and is believed to create a protective aura around the wearer. Select a symbol that resonates with you personally, as belief in its power can enhance its effectiveness. Wear the amulet as a necklace or carry it in your pocket, ready to grip it in moments of fear.

3. Dried Herbs (Sage, Rosemary, and Lavender)

Sage, rosemary, and lavender are commonly associated with protection and purification. Carry small sachets or bundles of these dried herbs as amulets to create a calming, protective energy around you. If you feel The Hugging Molly's approach, hold the herb close to your chest and inhale its scent, visualizing its energy as a shield. These herbs can also be burned in a safe location post-encounter to cleanse and release residual fear.

- **Using Sage:** Sage is particularly powerful for cleansing; you can carry a small stick of dried sage, and after an encounter, burn it carefully in a contained space to release any lingering energy.

4. Protective Stones (Obsidian, Amethyst, Black Tourmaline)

Certain stones and crystals are believed to absorb negative energy and protect against supernatural forces. Obsidian, amethyst, and black tourmaline are especially powerful, as they create grounding energy that can protect the mind and body. Carry a small stone in your pocket or wear it as a pendant. In an encounter, hold the stone tightly and visualize it absorbing her energy and deflecting it away from you.

5. Crosses and Religious Symbols

Crosses, rosaries, or other religious symbols can be effective if they hold personal meaning. These symbols provide psychological comfort and spiritual protection, reinforcing the belief in a higher power or force that protects against harm. If you wear a cross, hold it and repeat a protective prayer or affirmation if you sense her presence. The psychological impact of these symbols can strengthen your resilience and confidence.

6. Red String or Ribbon

In various folk traditions, a red string or ribbon tied around the wrist is believed to protect against negative energy and the "evil eye." This simple item is easy to wear and can be discreetly hidden under clothing. In moments of fear, touching the string can provide a sense of security, reminding you of the protection it symbolizes. Red is often associated with life force, energy, and resilience, making it a powerful color for symbolic protection.

Modern Gadgets That May Offer Protection or Warning

In addition to traditional items, modern gadgets can serve as protective tools by alerting you to changes in the environment or providing an added sense of security. The following devices can act as an early warning system or offer reassurance during encounters with supernatural forces.

1. EMF (Electromagnetic Field) Detector

An EMF detector can help identify unusual energy changes that may indicate the presence of supernatural entities. While this tool is commonly used in paranormal investigations, it can be useful for those venturing into areas where The Hugging Molly has been sighted. By monitoring changes in electromagnetic fields, an EMF detector can provide early warnings of supernatural activity, allowing you to prepare for a potential encounter.

- **Using an EMF Detector:** Hold the device steadily and move it slowly around your environment. Sudden spikes in EMF levels may signal an unusual presence, allowing you to make a quick exit if needed.

2. Thermal Camera or Infrared Thermometer

A thermal camera or infrared thermometer can detect sudden drops in temperature, which are often associated with supernatural activity. By monitoring cold spots, you can identify areas where her presence might be stronger. This tool provides a tangible indicator of environmental shifts, helping you confirm her proximity and decide whether to retreat.

3. Motion Sensor Lights

Portable motion sensor lights can be used to illuminate areas of high activity. Set up these lights along paths or in rooms where you sense her presence. When the light is triggered, it creates a break in the darkness, which may disrupt her approach. Motion lights are particularly useful in creating a boundary and giving you a momentary sense of control if she attempts to draw near.

4. Portable White Noise Generator

A portable white noise generator can help mask unsettling sounds, such as whispers or footsteps, providing mental relief. While it may not directly deter her, the constant background noise can reduce fear and increase focus. Choose a generator with adjustable volume and pitch, and use it to create a calming environment that keeps your nerves steady.

5. Digital Recorder

A digital voice recorder can capture sounds or voices that are often inaudible to the human ear. While it may not protect you directly, recording an encounter with The Hugging Molly can provide valuable information and evidence, allowing you to reflect on the experience afterward. This tool can also offer a sense of control, as focusing on documentation helps you stay grounded.

6. Handheld GPS Device

If you are exploring a known hotspot for sightings, a handheld GPS device can help you navigate safely and avoid getting lost. Many encounters occur in isolated areas where it is easy to lose direction, and a GPS can provide peace of mind, allowing you to focus on your surroundings without worrying about finding your way back. Use it to mark safe zones and routes back to populated areas.

Concluding Thoughts on Equipment for Protection

Protection against supernatural forces like The Hugging Molly requires a blend of traditional wisdom, modern technology, and psychological resilience. The items and tools discussed in this chapter provide both physical and spiritual safeguards, allowing you to enter potential hotspots with a sense of preparedness and confidence. By combining ancient symbols, natural elements, and advanced gadgets, you create a multi-layered defense that can help you navigate encounters with respect and control.

Chapter 12: Alternative Beliefs and Theories about The Hugging Molly

The legend of The Hugging Molly is enigmatic, and interpretations of her actions, motives, and even existence vary widely across different belief systems and cultural perspectives. These alternative beliefs and theories shed light on how people interpret her story, her intent, and the psychological and paranormal phenomena that may be at play. In this chapter, we'll explore the differing interpretations of The Hugging Molly's intent, examine parallels to other supernatural legends and cultural comparisons, and delve into psychological and paranormal theories that attempt to explain her nature and the experiences associated with her.

Differing Interpretations of Molly's Intent

The Hugging Molly's intent is a matter of debate, with theories ranging from interpretations of her as a malevolent spirit to a protective yet tragic figure. Each interpretation reflects different worldviews and adds nuance to her legend.

1. Molly as a Protective Spirit

One interpretation holds that The Hugging Molly is a protective spirit whose embrace is intended as a form of guidance rather than harm. In this view, her actions are seen as an attempt to keep individuals safe by frightening them away from danger. Some proponents of this theory suggest that she only approaches those who wander alone, especially at night, as a way of guiding them back to safety. Her embrace, while intimidating, can be seen as a warning against the risks of isolation and a reminder to heed communal wisdom about staying safe.

- **Supporting Evidence:** Many folklore figures serve as "cautionary guardians" who frighten people into good behavior, such as the bogeyman who keeps children indoors after dark. In cultures where oral tradition emphasizes caution, this protective interpretation of Molly's intent aligns with broader societal norms of communal protection.

2. Molly as a Tragic, Grieving Mother

A prevalent interpretation is that Molly is a figure of sorrow, haunted by the loss of her own child. In this view, her nightly wanderings and her eerie embrace are expressions of grief and longing, as she attempts to reconnect with what she has lost. The Hugging Molly may be seen as a restless spirit who has not found peace, bound by emotional pain that compels her to reach out to others in an effort to fill the void left by her loss.

- **Supporting Evidence:** Legends of grieving spirits, particularly female figures mourning lost children, are common in folklore worldwide. From La Llorona in Hispanic cultures to the banshee in Irish folklore, many cultures tell stories of maternal spirits seeking connection with the living to alleviate their sorrow.

3. Molly as a Vengeful Spirit

Some believe that The Hugging Molly is driven by anger or vengeance, particularly against those who wander into her domain. In this interpretation, her embrace is an act of aggression, a way of asserting dominance over those who dare to challenge her territory. Those who interpret her as vengeful suggest that her screams and constricting hug are meant to punish trespassers and enforce respect for her presence.

- **Supporting Evidence:** Folklore often includes "boundary spirits" or entities that protect their domain and punish those who enter without respect. Spirits like the Slavic Rusalka or the Japanese Yurei are believed to act vengefully toward those who trespass on their territory, making The Hugging Molly's aggressive embrace consistent with this archetype.

4. Molly as a Lost Soul in Search of Redemption

Some interpret The Hugging Molly's actions as those of a spirit seeking redemption or release from the mortal plane. In this view, she embraces lone travelers as a way of connecting with the living, possibly seeking help to "cross over" or find peace. This theory suggests that Molly's interactions are attempts to find solace or closure, relying on human connection as a means of emotional release.

- **Supporting Evidence:** Numerous ghost stories describe spirits bound to the physical realm due to unfinished business, often requiring assistance or acknowledgment to move on. Spirits seeking redemption are thought to haunt specific locations or people, hoping to find release through an act of compassion or understanding.

Parallels to Other Legends and Cultural Comparisons

The Hugging Molly is not an isolated figure in folklore; her story contains themes and elements that resonate across cultures. Examining these parallels offers insight into universal aspects of her legend and reveals the cultural significance of similar supernatural figures.

1. La Llorona (The Weeping Woman)

La Llorona, or "The Weeping Woman," is a well-known figure in Hispanic folklore. She is said to be the ghost of a woman who, in a fit of sorrow and madness, drowned her children and now roams rivers and lakes, crying for their return. La Llorona's story, like Molly's, contains themes of sorrow, maternal loss, and a longing for connection with the living. Both figures embody the archetype of the grieving mother, trapped in a cycle of remorse and sorrow.

- **Cultural Comparison:** Both The Hugging Molly and La Llorona serve as cautionary figures, warning people—especially children and young adults—of the dangers that lurk near rivers and isolated paths. Their grief and search for the lost make them relatable yet terrifying symbols of unresolved emotional trauma.

2. The Banshee of Irish Folklore

The banshee is a female spirit in Irish mythology, known for her mournful wailing, which is believed to be a harbinger of death. Like The Hugging Molly, the banshee has a powerful and unsettling scream that evokes fear. While the banshee does not physically interact with people as Molly does, both figures are associated with nighttime, eerie sounds, and a deep emotional impact on those who encounter them.

- **Cultural Comparison:** Both spirits are tied to the theme of warning, though the banshee warns of impending death, while The Hugging Molly may serve as a warning against isolation or wandering into dangerous areas alone. Each figure embodies the power of sound to create emotional resonance and caution.

3. The Bogeyman Archetype

The bogeyman, found in various cultures, is a creature used to frighten children into following rules or staying indoors. While the bogeyman's form and behavior vary widely, the general concept—a figure that enforces social norms through fear—closely aligns with certain interpretations of The Hugging Molly. Her story may have originated as a way to keep individuals from wandering alone at night, reinforcing communal expectations and safety.

- **Cultural Comparison:** Like the bogeyman, The Hugging Molly's role may be less about individual malevolence and more about social conditioning. By frightening people away from solitude or nighttime wandering, she fulfills a similar role, acting as a "guardian" of social norms and safety.

4. Japanese Yurei (Vengeful Spirits)

In Japanese folklore, Yurei are spirits of people who died with unresolved feelings, often returning to haunt those who wronged them or anyone who trespasses in their territory. Yurei are known for their intense emotional energy, which manifests as vengeful or sorrowful hauntings. Like The Hugging Molly, Yurei often appear in specific locations and are difficult to repel, driven by powerful emotions like sorrow or anger.

- **Cultural Comparison:** Both The Hugging Molly and Yurei are bound to particular places and act based on strong emotions. Their appearance is considered a cautionary experience, reflecting a universal belief in spirits who remain due to unfulfilled desires or unresolved trauma.

Psychological and Paranormal Theories

To understand The Hugging Molly, it is useful to explore both psychological and paranormal theories, each offering unique perspectives on her legend and the experiences people have reported.

1. Psychological Projection Theory

One psychological theory suggests that The Hugging Molly is a projection of deep-seated fears or traumas, particularly those related to isolation, abandonment, or grief. In this view, the legend acts as an external manifestation of internal emotions, especially for those dealing with loss or unresolved sorrow. For people facing these emotions, her presence may represent their struggle, with her hug embodying the weight of emotional burdens that they have yet to confront or process.

- **Explanation:** Projection theory posits that people externalize difficult feelings, turning them into external "threats" as a coping mechanism. The Hugging Molly's embrace can thus be seen as a symbolic experience of holding onto past grief or fears, giving them form through an external figure.

2. Mass Hysteria and Collective Memory

Some sociologists and psychologists believe that legends like The Hugging Molly can be partly attributed to mass hysteria and collective memory. When a story is repeated across generations, it may lead to collective belief, creating a "shared memory" that becomes real to those who believe in it. This collective memory builds over time, reinforcing the behaviors and phenomena associated with her.

- **Explanation:** The theory of mass hysteria suggests that when enough people believe in a phenomenon, it begins to manifest in ways that seem real. Witnesses may feel chills or see shadows simply due to their expectation, creating a cycle that validates the legend. This phenomenon shows how belief can generate real physical experiences, even if the source is psychological.

3. Residual Haunting Theory

In paranormal research, a "residual haunting" refers to the theory that certain locations capture emotional energy from past events, which can replay over time. If The Hugging Molly is seen in specific areas with a history of tragedy, her presence could be a form of residual energy—a lingering imprint rather than a conscious spirit. In this theory, Molly is not an aware entity but an echo, her actions repeating like a recording trapped in the physical space.

- **Explanation:** Residual haunting theory suggests that locations with high emotional impact can absorb and replay these energies. If Molly is an imprint rather than an active spirit, her embrace and scream could be "recordings" replaying through time, a haunting loop without awareness or intent.

4. Interdimensional Entity Theory

Some paranormal researchers theorize that entities like The Hugging Molly may originate from alternate dimensions or realities. Her interactions, including her touch and scream, could be interpreted as brief "crossings" between our dimension and another. In this view, she may not be a spirit of the dead but an interdimensional being whose actions are merely the natural way she perceives and interacts with humans in moments when the boundaries between dimensions overlap.

- **Explanation:** The interdimensional theory posits that certain times, locations, or emotional states allow beings from other dimensions to cross over briefly. The Hugging Molly's embrace might not be meant as fearsome in her realm, but rather a misunderstanding between dimensions, her actions misinterpreted by human witnesses.

5. Emotional Energy Attachment Theory

The concept of energy attachments suggests that spirits are drawn to individuals or places with specific emotional energy. If Molly is attracted to feelings of sadness, isolation, or anxiety, her presence may be triggered by individuals who resonate with her emotional state. In this theory, she seeks out people whose emotional frequency aligns with hers, and her embrace serves as a connection point rather than an attempt at harm.

- **Explanation:** Emotional energy theory posits that entities can be drawn to energies similar to their own, like a magnet. People experiencing loss or fear may unwittingly "call" her presence, aligning with her own emotions and facilitating an encounter.

Concluding Thoughts on Alternative Beliefs and Theories

The Hugging Molly's legend is multifaceted, and no single interpretation can fully explain her nature or intent. The theories and comparisons explored here highlight how her story resonates across cultures and how she reflects both universal fears and timeless mysteries. From psychological projections to interdimensional encounters, each theory provides a different lens, allowing us to better understand the complex tapestry of belief that surrounds her.

Chapter 13: Survival Stories of Encounters with The Hugging Molly

For generations, stories have circulated about encounters with The Hugging Molly. These firsthand accounts—some whispered in the dark, others passed down as family lore—offer valuable insights into her behavior, her approach, and how individuals have managed to endure and escape her infamous embrace. This chapter presents detailed survival stories, the lessons they offer, and how these real-life experiences can inform and prepare others. Each account sheds light on what to expect, highlighting effective strategies and warning against common mistakes, ultimately serving as a guide for anyone who might cross paths with this spectral figure.

Detailed Accounts from Those Who Survived Encounters

The following survival stories are based on accounts from individuals who claim to have encountered The Hugging Molly. Each story captures the unique aspects of the encounter, from the initial signs to the tactics employed, and the aftermath. These tales are presented as a resource for learning, equipping readers with firsthand knowledge of what it's like to face her and how survival is possible.

1. The Farmhand's Story – Abbeville, Alabama (1893)

In 1893, a young farmhand in Abbeville, Alabama, experienced a harrowing encounter while walking home after a long day's work. As he passed an abandoned house, he felt an overwhelming chill and heard footsteps behind him. Initially dismissing it as his imagination, he continued on his path until he felt a faint touch on his shoulder. When he turned, he found himself face-to-face with a tall, dark figure with outstretched arms.

- **Survival Tactics Used:** The farmhand managed to maintain eye contact and avoided panicking, choosing instead to back away slowly while murmuring, "I mean no harm." His calm, respectful tone seemed to dissuade The Hugging Molly from closing in completely. Instead of embracing him, she merely screamed, a sound that echoed for miles, and then vanished.

- **Lesson:** Remaining calm and using non-threatening body language may prevent a full embrace. Acknowledging her presence respectfully can reduce her perceived need to assert dominance.

2. The Hiker's Tale – Misty Valley, Texas (1987)

A young hiker exploring the trails near Misty Valley felt an eerie presence as dusk settled over the forest. She noticed an unnatural mist gathering around her, and soon afterward, she heard faint footsteps echoing through the trees. Recognizing the signs, she pulled out her flashlight and shone it around her, hoping to deter whatever presence might be lurking. Moments later, The Hugging Molly appeared in the mist, reaching toward her.

- **Survival Tactics Used:** The hiker used her flashlight to create a boundary between herself and Molly. She also used controlled breathing and focused on staying grounded, placing her hand on a tree to anchor herself. As Molly approached, the hiker spoke aloud, repeating, "I see you, I respect you," and took slow, deliberate steps backward. Eventually, Molly retreated, leaving her unharmed.

- **Lesson:** Using a flashlight as a boundary and anchoring oneself physically can help create a psychological shield. Speaking respectfully and moving deliberately may discourage a direct embrace.

3. The Widow's Encounter – Shadow Hollow, Louisiana (1921)

In the winter of 1921, an elderly widow in Shadow Hollow, Louisiana, experienced an encounter that would leave her shaken for years. On her way home one foggy night, she noticed a sudden drop in temperature and felt an intense, heavy silence around her. Suddenly, she sensed someone watching her, and before she could react, The Hugging Molly appeared and wrapped her in a tight embrace, pressing against her chest as if trying to convey something unspeakable.

- **Survival Tactics Used:** The widow, though frightened, chose to remain still, breathing as calmly as possible despite the intense pressure. She closed her eyes and began to pray softly, asking for peace for both herself and the spirit holding her. After several moments, Molly released her with a mournful cry and vanished into the mist.
- **Lesson:** Accepting rather than resisting the embrace, along with invoking a prayer or protective mantra, can sometimes reduce the intensity of her grip. Offering a sense of compassion or peace may lead to a swifter release.

4. The Teenager's Story – Raven's Peak, North Carolina (2002)

A teenager hiking in the dense woods of Raven's Peak heard stories of The Hugging Molly but never believed them until his own encounter one evening. He was heading back to camp when he felt a sudden chill, and the forest grew eerily quiet. Before he knew it, he felt hands on his shoulders, and her arms began to close around him.

- **Survival Tactics Used:** The teenager instinctively activated a personal alarm he had on hand, filling the air with loud, jarring noise. This seemed to startle Molly, who loosened her grip for a moment. He took the opportunity to break away, throwing salt behind him as he ran. The alarm, coupled with the salt, seemed to disrupt her, and she did not pursue him further.

- **Lesson:** Noise and salt can serve as powerful tools for self-defense, disrupting her approach and providing an opportunity to escape. Preparing in advance with physical deterrents like alarms and salt may allow a break from her grip.

5. The Fisherman's Encounter – Blackwater Creek, Louisiana (1956)

A fisherman from Blackwater Creek reported an encounter with The Hugging Molly while returning from an evening fishing trip. As he made his way home, he became aware of a dark figure following him along the narrow trail. The figure eventually approached him from behind, and before he could react, she wrapped him in an overwhelming embrace, freezing him in place.

- **Survival Tactics Used:** The fisherman kept his iron keychain close to his chest and mentally recited a personal mantra, "I am strong, I am here." The weight of the iron and the repetitive mantra seemed to steady him, and after a few moments, Molly's grip lessened, and she drifted away without further interaction.
- **Lesson:** Holding an iron object and repeating a personal mantra or affirmation can help maintain mental and physical resilience, potentially loosening her grip over time.

Lessons and Takeaways from Real-Life Experiences

These survival stories reveal consistent themes and lessons about how to navigate encounters with The Hugging Molly. Each account provides valuable strategies for responding to her presence, along with insights into behaviors that may de-escalate the encounter.

1. The Power of Respect and Acknowledgment

Acknowledging The Hugging Molly's presence calmly and respectfully appears to reduce her need to assert herself. Many survivors reported that maintaining eye contact, using respectful language, or quietly acknowledging her presence helped to de-escalate the encounter. This technique aligns with folklore beliefs that spirits seek acknowledgment without confrontation.

2. The Role of Physical Tools

The use of salt, flashlights, iron objects, and alarms proved effective in disrupting or deterring her approach. These tools serve as both psychological and physical barriers, providing a sense of control that can be crucial in high-stress situations. Preparing with these items can offer an advantage, creating boundaries that empower the individual and protect against supernatural influence.

3. Mindfulness and Mental Anchoring

Staying mindful, grounded, and centered was a common tactic among survivors. Techniques like deep breathing, focusing on sensory details, or repeating a mantra helped keep them mentally anchored, reducing fear and preventing panic. This mindfulness approach creates an internal boundary, reinforcing mental resilience and emotional stability during encounters.

4. Acceptance Over Resistance

In several cases, those who chose to accept the embrace, rather than struggle against it, reported a faster release. Resisting can heighten the intensity of the encounter, as struggling often increases her grip. Accepting the experience and mentally focusing on calmness or peace appears to soothe her presence, leading to a less distressing interaction.

How These Stories Can Inform and Prepare Others

The firsthand accounts of encounters with The Hugging Molly offer more than just cautionary tales; they provide a roadmap for preparation and survival. By learning from these stories, others can approach similar experiences with knowledge and resilience, equipped with effective strategies and an understanding of what to expect.

1. Anticipate and Recognize Early Signs

Survivors consistently reported chills, sudden silence, or footsteps as early warning signs. Recognizing these signs allows individuals to mentally prepare and implement protective measures before her approach. Knowing what to expect reduces the element of surprise, empowering potential witnesses to respond thoughtfully.

2. Prepare with Tools and Protective Items

Each account highlights the importance of carrying protective tools like flashlights, salt, iron, or personal alarms. By equipping oneself with these items, individuals can create layers of defense, giving them practical and psychological advantages. Preparing with these tools reinforces self-assurance, helping individuals feel more secure during encounters.

3. Use Calming Techniques to Maintain Composure

Calming techniques such as deep breathing, mantra repetition, and grounding exercises can make a significant difference in managing fear. Learning and practicing these techniques in advance enables individuals to respond from a place of calm, reducing the impact of panic and maintaining control even when faced with a supernatural force.

4. Embrace Knowledge as Empowerment

Stories of survival demonstrate that knowledge itself is a powerful tool. By studying the accounts of others, potential witnesses gain insight into effective tactics and common mistakes, allowing them to enter potential encounters with a calm, prepared mindset. Understanding The Hugging Molly's behaviors and how others have survived her embrace can reduce fear, transforming the experience into one of resilience.

Concluding Thoughts on Survival Stories

The survival stories presented in this chapter remind us that encounters with The Hugging Molly, while terrifying, are survivable. Through a combination of mental preparation, respectful acknowledgment, practical tools, and calming techniques, individuals have endured her presence and emerged unscathed. These real-life experiences offer a blueprint for others, transforming fear into informed action.

Chapter 14: Debunking Myths Surrounding The Hugging Molly

The Hugging Molly has become a deeply rooted figure in folklore, with her story evolving over generations. As with any legend, facts and myths intertwine, creating misconceptions that can obscure the original essence of her tale. This chapter aims to separate fact from fiction, examining the origins of common myths about The Hugging Molly and exploring how myth and truth are intertwined in her legend. By debunking these myths, we gain a clearer understanding of who—or what—The Hugging Molly might truly be, and the cultural truths her story reflects.

Separating Fact from Fiction in The Hugging Molly Lore

Many aspects of The Hugging Molly's story have been embellished, altered, or misunderstood over time. Some of these changes arose as the legend spread, while others may have been influenced by cultural beliefs and psychological interpretations. Here, we take a closer look at what is most likely factual versus fictional within her lore.

1. The Hugging Molly as a Real Historical Figure

One of the most persistent beliefs is that The Hugging Molly was once a real woman who lived in Abbeville, Alabama, in the 19th century, with her spirit continuing to haunt the area. According to this version, she was a grieving mother who lost her child under tragic circumstances, and her spirit now roams in search of solace. While there is no verifiable historical record of a woman named Molly meeting such a fate, this belief remains popular due to its emotional resonance and its grounding in real human experiences of grief.

- **Fact Check:** Although the story may have been inspired by real figures or local tragedies, there is no documented evidence of a specific woman named Molly in Abbeville who suffered such a loss. This aspect of the story appears to be more of a symbolic narrative than a literal historical account.

2. The Hugging Molly as a Malevolent Spirit

Over time, some have come to view The Hugging Molly as a vengeful or malevolent spirit, believing that she actively seeks to harm those she encounters. Stories often depict her grip as suffocating and her scream as paralyzing, leading people to assume that she is an inherently dangerous entity. This view has led to the myth that she harms her victims, which has added an element of fear to the legend that may not align with her original intent.

- **Fact Check:** While her appearance is frightening and her grip intense, there are no accounts of The Hugging Molly physically injuring or causing permanent harm to those she encounters. Most witnesses describe her as intimidating, but there is no evidence to support the notion of her as malevolent or violent. The fear associated with her likely stems from her unsettling presence rather than any malicious intent.

3. The Idea that She Only Targets the Young

A widespread misconception is that The Hugging Molly exclusively targets children or young adults, leading many to associate her with the bogeyman archetype. This perception may stem from the protective aspects of her legend, which serve as a warning for young people not to wander alone at night. However, historical accounts include encounters with adults of various ages, suggesting that she may appear to anyone who fits certain behavioral or emotional patterns.

- **Fact Check:** The Hugging Molly has been known to approach individuals of all ages, and her appearances are not limited to children. While her story has likely been used as a cautionary tale for young people, she seems to appear to those who are vulnerable, alone, or emotionally receptive, rather than focusing exclusively on age.

4. Her Embrace as a Physical Threat

The intensity of The Hugging Molly's embrace has often been exaggerated in modern retellings, with some claiming that her hug is physically crushing or capable of causing suffocation. This myth likely originates from the experience of overwhelming fear, which can make her grip feel constrictive or even paralyzing. Over time, her hug has come to be associated with physical harm, although no verified account describes her embrace as life-threatening.

- **Fact Check:** Her embrace may feel intense or immobilizing, but it does not seem to cause physical injury. The feeling of suffocation is likely psychological, rooted in fear and the unexpected nature of her touch rather than any true physical harm.

5. Her Scream as a Curse or Spell

Some believe that The Hugging Molly's scream is a curse that haunts victims, leaving them marked or destined for misfortune. This belief may be tied to cultural fears about supernatural sounds, which are often seen as omens. While her scream is described as unsettling and even chilling, there is no evidence to support the idea that it has long-term effects or that it carries any specific curse.

- **Fact Check:** Her scream is likely an emotional or supernatural expression of her presence, not a form of curse or spell. Most accounts indicate that the scream is frightening but without lasting supernatural repercussions. This aspect of the myth appears to stem from cultural fears about ghostly sounds rather than any specific ability she possesses.

Common Misconceptions and Their Origins

As with many legends, certain misconceptions have developed around The Hugging Molly's story, often influenced by cultural beliefs, psychological interpretations, or embellishments. Here, we explore the origins of these misconceptions and how they shape the way people perceive her.

1. Association with Other Malevolent Spirits

The Hugging Molly is often associated with malicious spirits or demons due to her dark figure and intense presence. In some retellings, she has been equated with demonic entities who prey on the vulnerable. This misconception likely arose from a blend of folk beliefs and supernatural archetypes, where spirits that appear at night or evoke fear are often categorized as malevolent. Additionally, human fear of the unknown can lead people to ascribe malevolence to figures they do not fully understand.

- **Origin:** This misconception stems from general fears of the supernatural and the human tendency to categorize all night-dwelling spirits as threatening. The archetype of the "dark figure" often signifies danger, leading people to assume a harmful intent that may not actually be present in The Hugging Molly's behavior.

2. Comparison with the Bogeyman

Due to her role in cautioning individuals against wandering alone, The Hugging Molly is frequently likened to the bogeyman—a figure that parents often use to keep children indoors. This comparison has led many to believe that she only appears to frighten children, reinforcing the idea that her purpose is to enforce social rules rather than engage with adults.

- **Origin:** The bogeyman comparison likely originated from parents who used her story as a way to keep young people safe at night. While her actions do encourage caution, her story has broader implications beyond the scope of keeping children from wandering.

3. Interpretation as a Woman in Mourning

The idea that The Hugging Molly is a grieving mother searching for her lost child is one of the most persistent interpretations of her story. While this interpretation provides a compelling emotional dimension, it is also largely speculative. This story likely originated from the cultural archetype of the grieving mother, which is found in many legends, and it helps humanize her actions, framing her embrace as an expression of sorrow rather than malice.

- **Origin:** This myth may have originated as a way to explain her behavior empathetically, aligning with universal themes of loss and maternal love. Her actions, such as reaching out to those who wander alone, could be interpreted as attempts to reconnect with what she has lost, making her story relatable.

4. Misconception About Physical Weakness

Some believe that she can be easily repelled with physical actions, such as pushing her away or breaking free from her grip. This misconception may come from the desire to rationalize her presence in physical terms, assuming that typical physical self-defense tactics can work. However, those who have encountered her often report that her strength is supernatural, and resistance tends to provoke a stronger response.

- **Origin:** The belief in physical defense likely stems from a natural inclination to apply real-world logic to supernatural encounters. While physical movements like grounding or controlled steps can help, direct physical resistance often has the opposite effect, as she does not adhere to human physical limitations.

5. Idea That She Only Appears on Certain Nights or Phases of the Moon

Some believe that The Hugging Molly only appears during certain phases of the moon, such as a full moon, or on specific nights of the year. This idea is often associated with beliefs about the supernatural being more active during specific lunar phases. While many accounts describe nighttime sightings, there is no clear pattern in her appearances based on lunar phases or specific dates.

- **Origin:** This belief likely comes from broader cultural superstitions about the supernatural being tied to lunar cycles. The fear of the full moon and other lunar phases has long been associated with heightened paranormal activity, although there is no clear evidence that The Hugging Molly's appearances are bound to these cycles.

How Myth and Truth Intertwine in the Legend

The intertwining of myth and truth in The Hugging Molly's story reflects the way human imagination and collective memory shape folklore. Myths serve as cultural markers, adding depth and moral lessons, while the core truths about her behavior and appearance remain constant. This blend of myth and truth is what keeps her story alive, relevant, and evolving.

1. The Role of Emotion in Shaping the Legend

Emotion is central to the evolution of The Hugging Molly's story. Her association with grief, fear, and protection speaks to universal emotional experiences, which have been woven into the fabric of her legend. The idea of a mother searching for her lost child, for instance, resonates because it taps into a common emotional reality. Even if untrue in a literal sense, this aspect of the story provides a relatable and compassionate perspective on her actions.

2. Cultural Norms and Social Caution

Myths surrounding The Hugging Molly often reflect cultural values, especially regarding safety, communal respect, and protection of the vulnerable. Her story serves as a cautionary tale about the risks of isolation and the importance of respecting certain boundaries. By embodying these cultural values, the legend reinforces social norms, blending caution with supernatural fear to instill a respect for communal wisdom.

3. Interpretation as an Archetype of the Unknown

The Hugging Molly's mysterious nature reflects human fascination with the unknown. Her undefined motives and unpredictable behavior leave room for interpretation, allowing each generation to add its own layer to the story. The ambiguity of her character invites speculation, and as myths accumulate, they create a fuller picture that speaks to the primal human need to understand—and sometimes fear—the unknown.

4. Evolution Through Storytelling

The Hugging Molly's legend has evolved through storytelling, with each retelling introducing slight variations that enhance her mystique. This evolution reflects the adaptability of folklore; as societal fears and values shift, so too does the way people perceive her. Myths about her intentions, powers, and vulnerabilities adapt to contemporary beliefs, creating a legend that is both timeless and ever-changing.

Concluding Thoughts on Debunking Myths

Separating fact from fiction in The Hugging Molly's story allows us to better understand the cultural, emotional, and psychological underpinnings of her legend. While some aspects of her story are rooted in universal archetypes and cautionary tales, others are shaped by the way people interpret and adapt her narrative to their own lives. By debunking myths, we gain a clearer picture of The Hugging Molly, recognizing her as both a figure of fear and a symbol that reflects our own experiences and cultural beliefs.

Chapter 15: First Aid for Post-Encounter Trauma

Surviving an encounter with The Hugging Molly can leave lasting effects, both physically and emotionally. While her embrace may not result in serious physical injuries, the psychological impact can be profound, often leading to lingering fear, anxiety, and even post-traumatic stress. This chapter offers detailed guidance on first aid for post-encounter trauma, focusing on immediate recovery steps, physical and emotional healing techniques, and resources for long-term coping with fear and trauma. By understanding how to manage the aftermath of an encounter, individuals can reclaim their sense of safety, regain emotional balance, and integrate the experience into a resilient, empowered self.

Physical and Emotional Recovery Tips

Encounters with The Hugging Molly can produce intense physical and emotional responses. Whether you've experienced her chilling presence, her scream, or the restrictive pressure of her embrace, it's essential to prioritize recovery to prevent prolonged trauma. The following tips address both the physical and emotional aspects of recovery.

Physical Recovery Tips

1. Grounding Exercises

Grounding exercises help reconnect you with the physical world, reminding you that you are safe and present. Simple grounding techniques can calm the nervous system and reduce lingering sensations from the encounter. Try the **5-4-3-2-1 grounding method**:

- Identify five things you can see around you.
- Name four things you can touch.
- Listen for three sounds you can hear.
- Notice two things you can smell.

• Identify one thing you can taste.

This exercise can ease the transition from the encounter back into reality, grounding your senses and bringing your mind back to the present.

2.Controlled Breathing

Encounters with The Hugging Molly can lead to shallow or erratic breathing, a common response to fear. Controlled breathing helps re-regulate the body, stabilizing heart rate and calming the nervous system. One effective method is the **4-7-8 technique**:

- Inhale through your nose for four counts.
- Hold your breath for seven counts.
- Exhale through your mouth for eight counts.

This technique can be done immediately after the encounter to regain control and can be repeated as needed to reduce anxiety.

3.Muscle Relaxation Techniques

Her embrace often induces physical tension, particularly in the shoulders, chest, and arms. To alleviate this tension, try **progressive muscle relaxation**:

- Start by tensing each muscle group for five seconds, then release.
- Begin with your toes, then move to your calves, thighs, abdomen, chest, arms, and face.
- Consciously release the tension with each exhale.

This technique helps relax the muscles, releases any residual tension from the encounter, and provides physical relief.

4.Soothing Aromatherapy

Essential oils can offer a sense of calm and aid in physical relaxation. Lavender, chamomile, and frankincense are especially helpful for calming the body and mind. Place a few drops on your wrists or inhale from a handkerchief. Aromatherapy can create a sense of safety and comfort, reducing anxiety and promoting relaxation after a distressing experience.

Emotional Recovery Tips

1. Acknowledge the Fear

Acknowledging the fear you experienced, rather than suppressing it, is an important step toward processing the encounter. Remind yourself that fear is a natural response and that feeling unsettled is normal. Journaling about the experience can help release pent-up emotions, allowing you to articulate your feelings and begin the healing process.

1. Practice Mindful Observation

Mindfulness allows you to observe your thoughts without judgment. Sit quietly, close your eyes, and allow any memories of the encounter to surface. Rather than analyzing or reliving the event, simply acknowledge each thought and let it pass. Practicing mindfulness helps create emotional distance, allowing you to integrate the experience without being overwhelmed by it.

2.Develop a Personal Mantra

Create a calming mantra that reinforces your sense of safety and resilience. Repeating phrases like "I am safe now," or "This experience does not control me," can reinforce positive, calming thoughts. Mantras work by shifting the focus from fear to empowerment, reconditioning the mind to associate the encounter with inner strength rather than helplessness.

3.Engage in Gentle Physical Activity

Light activities, such as walking, stretching, or yoga, can help process residual fear and stress by releasing endorphins and improving circulation. Physical movement allows the body to release stored tension, creating a sense of emotional relief. Gentle exercise, especially in nature, can also promote mental clarity and relaxation, easing the mind after a high-stress encounter.

Immediate Actions to Take Post-Escape

Taking quick, intentional actions after escaping an encounter with The Hugging Molly can prevent trauma from deepening and help restore a sense of control. Here are steps to consider immediately after leaving her presence.

1. Find a Safe, Comfortable Space

Locate a place where you feel physically and emotionally secure. If possible, choose a well-lit area with people around, such as a friend's home, a public park, or a familiar room in your own home. Familiar, comfortable spaces can help you re-establish safety and reduce feelings of vulnerability.

2. Communicate with a Trusted Person

Talk to someone you trust about the experience, whether a friend, family member, or counselor. Verbalizing the encounter can help reduce its intensity, allowing you to process the fear with someone who can provide reassurance and perspective. If in-person support isn't possible, consider calling a supportive person or journaling about the experience.

3. Apply Calming Touch or Self-Hug

Applying a calming touch can ground you and reduce anxiety. Place your hand over your chest or wrap your arms around yourself, mimicking a self-hug. This gentle touch can provide comfort and reinforce your personal boundaries, creating a safe space within your body. If possible, use a soft blanket or item that brings comfort to enhance the sense of security.

4.Use a Warm Compress or Drink a Warm Beverage

A warm compress on your chest or neck can relax muscles and comfort the nervous system. Alternatively, drinking a warm beverage like herbal tea can have a calming effect. The warmth soothes the body, which signals safety to the mind, helping you release residual anxiety from the encounter.

5.Reaffirm Boundaries with Visualizations

Visualizations can re-establish a sense of control by reinforcing boundaries. Imagine a protective barrier surrounding you, one that keeps you safe from any lingering energies. Envision this boundary growing stronger and brighter with each breath, solidifying your sense of personal space and security.

Resources for Coping with Fear and Trauma

The emotional impact of an encounter with The Hugging Molly can be lasting, and many people benefit from resources and strategies to help process the trauma. The following tools and resources are designed to support emotional recovery and prevent lingering fear from taking hold.

1. Therapeutic Journaling

Journaling provides a structured way to process and release emotions. Consider keeping a specific journal for the experience, documenting each aspect of the encounter and how you felt before, during, and afterward. Writing down your thoughts can help transform the experience from an overwhelming memory into an organized narrative, providing a sense of closure.

- **Prompts for Post-Encounter Journaling:**
    - "What physical sensations did I experience, and how did they change over time?"
    - "What emotions arose during and after the encounter?"
    - "What strengths did I discover within myself during this experience?"

2. Grounding and Meditation Apps

Many apps provide guided meditations and grounding exercises specifically designed for anxiety and stress relief. Apps like **Calm**, **Headspace**, and **Insight Timer** offer programs that focus on mindful breathing, visualization, and emotional recovery, helping you regain control and calm after an encounter.

- **Suggested Meditation Topics:**
    - Managing fear and anxiety
    - Visualizations for safety and grounding
    - Techniques for emotional release and letting go

3. Breathing Exercises for Anxiety Relief

Practicing breathing exercises regularly can help manage anxiety and prevent lingering trauma from taking root. Techniques such as diaphragmatic breathing (belly breathing) and box breathing are particularly effective in calming the mind. Developing a daily practice of these techniques can make them second nature, so they're readily available if anxiety resurfaces.

- **Box Breathing Technique:**
  - Inhale for four counts, hold for four counts, exhale for four counts, hold for four counts, then repeat.

4. Cognitive Behavioral Therapy (CBT) Techniques

Cognitive Behavioral Therapy (CBT) is a highly effective approach for managing anxiety and trauma by identifying and changing negative thought patterns. Working with a mental health professional trained in CBT can help you reshape fears around the encounter, replacing fear-based thinking with empowering, realistic perspectives.

- **Basic CBT Approach to Fear:**
  - Identify the fear-based thoughts associated with the encounter.
  - Challenge the irrational beliefs behind these thoughts.
  - Replace them with balanced, realistic alternatives, like "I am safe now" or "I survived this and can continue to overcome."

5. Joining Support Groups or Online Communities

Sharing experiences with others who have faced similar encounters can be deeply validating and therapeutic. Consider joining support groups, either in person or online, to discuss your encounter and hear stories from others. Connecting with others can reduce feelings of isolation, reinforcing that you are not alone in your experience.

- **Online Platforms for Sharing Experiences:**
    - Paranormal forums and safe spaces for encounter discussions.
    - Support groups on social media platforms.
    - Online communities focused on supernatural experiences and resilience.

6. Creative Expression for Emotional Release

Artistic expression—whether drawing, painting, music, or writing—can be an outlet for the emotional aftermath of an encounter. Expressing your experience through art can help externalize emotions, making them easier to process. Creating something tangible out of the intangible experience provides a sense of control and closure, transforming fear into creative empowerment.

Concluding Thoughts on First Aid for Post-Encounter Trauma

Recovering from an encounter with The Hugging Molly involves addressing both physical and emotional needs, re-establishing a sense of safety, and allowing time to heal. By using practical grounding techniques, expressing emotions, and accessing available resources, survivors can move beyond the fear and integrate the experience as a testament to resilience. Trauma does not have to define the aftermath; instead, it can be an opportunity to cultivate inner strength, reclaim personal space, and transform fear into a newfound sense of courage and self-assurance.

In reflecting on all that has been explored, remember that these encounters—while unsettling—can offer profound lessons in resilience, self-discovery, and the mysteries of the human experience.

Chapter 16: Seeking Professional Help and Support After an Encounter

An encounter with The Hugging Molly, or any supernatural experience, can have lasting psychological effects. For some, the fear, confusion, and trauma may fade with time and self-care; for others, professional help is essential to process the experience and fully recover. This chapter provides guidance on when to seek expert assistance, how to access mental health resources, and the support available through organizations and community networks. Understanding that you don't have to face the aftermath alone can empower you to reclaim your peace of mind, helping you transform fear into resilience with the support of qualified professionals and compassionate communities.

When and How to Involve Experts or Support Groups

Seeking professional help or joining support groups can be immensely beneficial, especially when self-care techniques are not enough. Knowing when to involve experts is crucial in managing post-encounter trauma, so recognizing the signs that professional support may be necessary can help ensure effective healing.

1. Recognizing Signs that Professional Help May Be Needed

Encounters with supernatural entities can impact people in complex ways, and the need for help can vary widely based on individual responses. If you experience any of the following, it may be time to reach out to a mental health professional or support group:

- **Persistent Anxiety or Fear:** If you continue to feel anxious, hypervigilant, or fearful long after the encounter, professional support may be needed to address these feelings and prevent them from affecting daily life.
- **Recurring Nightmares or Flashbacks:** Frequent dreams, flashbacks, or intrusive thoughts related to the encounter are signs of post-traumatic stress. Therapy can help you process these memories and reduce their impact.

- **Difficulty Returning to Normal Routines:** If the encounter disrupts your ability to work, socialize, or participate in daily activities, a mental health professional can provide strategies for regaining a sense of normalcy.
- **Emotional Numbness or Detachment:** Emotional numbness, detachment from loved ones, or an inability to feel joy are common responses to trauma. Seeking help can provide you with tools to reconnect emotionally.
- **Panic Attacks or Physical Symptoms of Anxiety:** Physical symptoms, such as heart palpitations, shortness of breath, or panic attacks, may indicate lingering trauma. Therapy can offer coping mechanisms to manage these symptoms.

2. Types of Professionals to Consider

There are various mental health professionals who can provide specialized support based on your needs. Understanding the different options can help you make an informed choice.

- **Licensed Therapists and Counselors:** Therapists and counselors provide a safe space for talking through your experiences, exploring emotions, and learning coping strategies. They specialize in various therapeutic approaches, such as Cognitive Behavioral Therapy (CBT) and trauma-focused therapy, which are effective for anxiety and fear management.
- **Psychologists:** Psychologists are trained to diagnose mental health conditions and offer various types of therapy, including specialized approaches for post-traumatic stress and anxiety. If the encounter has left you feeling overwhelmed, psychologists can provide structured treatment plans.
- **Psychiatrists:** If the experience has triggered intense, long-lasting symptoms, psychiatrists can evaluate you for medication support to stabilize anxiety, insomnia, or panic attacks. Medication is

typically used as part of a broader treatment plan and can be helpful when symptoms are severe.

- **Trauma Specialists:** Trauma specialists are mental health professionals with specific training in trauma recovery. They understand the complexities of traumatic experiences, including supernatural encounters, and can offer a safe, understanding approach to healing.

- **Support Group Facilitators:** Many support groups are led by facilitators trained to guide discussions in a safe and supportive manner. They can provide peer support and help normalize your experience, fostering healing through shared understanding.

3. How to Approach Seeking Support

Starting the process of finding support can feel daunting, especially after a supernatural encounter. Here are practical steps to help you initiate this journey:

- **Research and Reach Out:** Begin by researching therapists, counselors, or trauma specialists in your area. Websites like **Psychology Today**, **Therapist Finder**, and **GoodTherapy** allow you to filter by specialty and location. Online therapy options, like **BetterHelp** and **Talkspace**, are also accessible from home.

- **Consider Your Needs:** Think about whether you prefer in-person sessions or feel more comfortable with virtual therapy. Some people find comfort in discussing supernatural experiences with those who specialize in trauma or even paranormal psychology, which may be available in certain regions.

- **Prepare for Your First Session:** When contacting a therapist, be open about your reason for seeking support. You might say, "I had a distressing experience that I'm struggling to process, and I'd like support managing my anxiety and fear."

- **Join Support Groups:** If individual therapy isn't feasible, look for support groups, either online or in your community. Support groups provide a safe space to discuss experiences with people who may have faced similar situations.

Resources for Mental Health Assistance

Numerous resources are available to help you find mental health support, including therapy directories, helplines, and organizations specializing in trauma recovery. Each resource provides different levels of assistance, so you can find the support that best fits your needs.

1. Online Therapy Platforms

Online therapy platforms allow you to access licensed professionals from the comfort of home, which can be especially helpful if you are dealing with lingering fear or anxiety. Here are popular options:

- **BetterHelp:** An online platform offering licensed therapists who specialize in various mental health needs, including anxiety, trauma, and stress. Sessions are conducted via video, phone, or messaging.
- **Talkspace:** Provides therapy sessions through messaging, video, and phone calls. Talkspace connects you with licensed therapists who can help with post-trauma coping and anxiety management.
- **Regain:** An online therapy platform specifically for couples and individuals dealing with relationship-based stress or trauma, which may be beneficial if the encounter affected your ability to connect with others.

2. Helplines and Crisis Resources

For immediate support, mental health helplines offer free and confidential assistance. Helplines provide access to trained counselors and can help direct you to further resources.

- **National Alliance on Mental Illness (NAMI) Helpline:** Offers free mental health support and referrals in the United States. Call 1-800-950-NAMI (6264).

- **Crisis Text Line:** A 24/7 crisis line offering text-based support. Text "HELLO" to 741741 in the United States for immediate support with anxiety, panic, or post-traumatic stress.
- **SAMHSA National Helpline:** The Substance Abuse and Mental Health Services Administration offers a helpline for those in crisis and needing support. Call 1-800-662-HELP (4357) in the United States for assistance and referrals to trauma counselors.

3. National and Local Mental Health Organizations

Many organizations offer resources, counseling, and information on trauma recovery. These organizations provide guidance on finding therapists, self-help strategies, and online communities.

- **American Psychological Association (APA):** The APA provides a directory of licensed therapists, along with educational resources on trauma recovery and mental health.
- **National Center for PTSD:** A resource for individuals dealing with post-traumatic stress. They offer educational materials, self-help tools, and guidance on finding specialized trauma support.
- **Anxiety and Depression Association of America (ADAA):** Offers resources and information on finding treatment for anxiety, trauma, and related mental health concerns, including tools for managing fear and coping with trauma.

4. Apps and Digital Mental Health Tools

Apps designed for mental health support offer self-guided tools for managing anxiety, stress, and trauma symptoms. These tools can complement therapy and provide additional support between sessions.

- **Calm:** Offers guided meditations, sleep stories, and breathing exercises to alleviate anxiety and stress. Calm's resources can be particularly helpful for managing post-encounter fear and regaining relaxation.

- **Headspace:** Provides mindfulness training and meditation exercises. Headspace's grounding techniques can assist in creating a sense of safety and reducing anxiety from the encounter.
- **Insight Timer:** A free meditation app that includes a wide range of meditations specifically for trauma recovery, anxiety management, and grounding techniques.

Organizations and Community Support Networks

Connecting with support networks can provide a sense of community and understanding, offering reassurance that others have faced similar experiences. These organizations and networks provide group-based support, community resources, and connections to others who have encountered similar supernatural or traumatic events.

1. Paranormal Support Groups

Paranormal support groups provide a unique space to discuss supernatural encounters without judgment. These groups often attract individuals who have experienced the unexplained and provide community support for processing such events. Look for groups in your area or join online paranormal forums.

- **International Paranormal Society (IPS):** The IPS provides support networks for individuals who have experienced paranormal events, including local chapter groups and online discussions.
- **Ghost Research Society (GRS):** The GRS offers resources and community support for those who have had encounters with supernatural entities. They provide a safe space for sharing experiences and learning about paranormal investigations.

2. Community Centers and Peer Support Groups

Community centers often host peer support groups, where you can discuss personal experiences in a safe, welcoming environment. Peer support groups offer emotional support and a sense of camaraderie, helping you feel less isolated.

- **Local Community Centers:** Many community centers offer support groups for anxiety and trauma. Check your local center's website or bulletin board for group listings.
- **Faith-Based Organizations:** For those who find comfort in spiritual or faith-based support, local churches, temples, or synagogues often offer counseling and support groups focused on emotional resilience and healing.

3. Online Supernatural Encounter Communities

Several online communities are dedicated to discussing supernatural experiences. These forums provide a safe, anonymous way to share your story and connect with others who have encountered similar entities.

- **Reddit (r/Paranormal and r/UnresolvedMysteries):** These subreddits offer a space for people to share their supernatural experiences and receive support, insights, and coping strategies from others in the community.
- **True Ghost Stories (Website and Forum):** This online community is dedicated to sharing true ghost stories, providing a platform for sharing encounters and gaining validation from people with similar experiences.
- **Your Ghost Stories (Website):** An online forum where users can post their supernatural encounters and receive feedback and support from other community members.

Concluding Thoughts on Seeking Professional Help and Support

Recovering from an encounter with The Hugging Molly is a journey, one that may require more than personal resilience alone. Knowing when to seek professional help or join a support network can provide the guidance and understanding needed to fully process the experience, reducing the potential for lingering fear and trauma. Whether through individual therapy, group support, or online communities, accessing external resources offers a path toward healing, empowerment, and emotional stability.

Ultimately, seeking support demonstrates strength and a commitment to personal growth, transforming fear into a source of resilience. In choosing to face and process the encounter with compassionate guidance, individuals can reclaim their inner peace, using the experience to cultivate a deeper understanding of both the supernatural and their own capacity for healing.

Chapter 17: How to Share Your Story Safely

Sharing a supernatural encounter, such as one with The Hugging Molly, can be a powerful step toward healing and understanding. However, it also requires sensitivity, respect, and a clear understanding of the potential impacts on yourself and others. This chapter provides detailed guidance on safely and responsibly sharing your story, covering tips for effectively communicating your experience, respecting others' beliefs and boundaries, and considering the possible consequences of making your story public. Whether through writing, online communities, or in-person conversations, telling your story can be a meaningful way to process the encounter while offering support to others with similar experiences.

Tips on Writing or Sharing Your Experience Responsibly

When recounting a supernatural experience, whether through writing or speaking, it's essential to approach the story with intention and care. Below are strategies to help you share your story in a way that is honest, mindful, and effective.

1. Set Your Intentions for Sharing

Clarifying why you want to share your story can help you focus on the purpose of your recount. Consider the reasons behind your desire to share: Is it to process the experience, offer guidance to others, seek validation, or contribute to discussions around supernatural phenomena? Understanding your goals can help you determine the best way to frame your story.

- **Examples of Intentions:** "I want to share to help others who have faced similar experiences feel less alone," or "I want to document my encounter to process my own feelings and gain closure."

2. Choose the Right Medium for Your Comfort

How you share your story can influence the level of control you have over how it's received. Consider whether you feel more comfortable writing a personal journal entry, sharing on an anonymous online forum, speaking in a support group, or publishing your story more publicly.

- **Personal Journaling:** Offers privacy and a safe space for processing emotions.
- **Anonymous Online Forums:** Provide community validation with the option of remaining anonymous.
- **Support Groups:** Allow for face-to-face support with people who are often more open to supernatural experiences.
- **Public Blogging or Social Media:** Gives your story visibility but requires thoughtful consideration of potential reactions.

3. Be Clear and Objective in Describing Events

When recounting supernatural experiences, clarity can help others understand what you went through without embellishment or ambiguity. Describe what happened as objectively as possible, focusing on the specifics of the experience (time, place, physical sensations, emotions) to make your account relatable and authentic.

- **Example:** Instead of saying, "I felt like I was being suffocated by pure evil," try "I felt a tightening around my chest and a profound sense of dread. My heart raced, and I found it hard to breathe."

4. Acknowledge Both Facts and Feelings

Balancing factual recounting with emotional processing can make your story more relatable. Clearly distinguish between what happened and how you felt, as this helps readers or listeners separate the event from the impact, allowing them to empathize without judgment.

- **Example Statement:** "The encounter left me feeling vulnerable and scared, even though I was physically unharmed."

5. Use Disclaimers or Trigger Warnings

Supernatural encounters can evoke fear and anxiety in some readers or listeners, so it's respectful to add disclaimers or trigger warnings. This gives others the chance to choose whether they want to proceed with reading or listening to potentially distressing material.

- **Example Disclaimer:** "Warning: This story contains descriptions of a supernatural experience that may be unsettling for some readers."

6. Invite Open Dialogue or Feedback if Desired

If you're comfortable receiving feedback, encourage open dialogue by asking readers or listeners to share their thoughts respectfully. Inviting feedback can help foster a sense of community and support. If feedback feels overwhelming, consider limiting where and how people can respond, such as allowing comments only in a moderated forum.

- **Example:** "If you've had a similar experience, feel free to share in the comments, or reach out directly if you'd like to discuss privately."

Respect for Others' Beliefs and Fears

When sharing a story involving supernatural themes, it's essential to remain respectful of others' diverse beliefs and fears. Understanding and honoring these differences can make your story more approachable and create a safe space for those with varying perspectives.

1. Acknowledge Different Belief Systems

People interpret supernatural experiences in vastly different ways. Some may see them as spiritual encounters, while others may view them through psychological, scientific, or skeptical lenses. Acknowledging these perspectives can prevent alienating your audience and helps maintain a respectful tone.

- **Example Statement:** "I understand that everyone has different beliefs about the supernatural, and I'm sharing my experience as it happened to me, without expecting others to agree or believe in the same way."

2. Avoid Imposing Your Interpretation as Universal Truth

While sharing your perspective is natural, framing it as the only valid interpretation can be off-putting for those with different beliefs. Presenting your experience as personal rather than universal allows others to interpret it according to their worldview.

- **Example Statement:** "This is how I interpreted my experience with The Hugging Molly. Others may see it differently, and I respect those perspectives."

3. Be Sensitive to Potentially Triggering Content

Some individuals may find discussions of supernatural encounters distressing or triggering. When sharing your story in detail, especially in a group setting, try to gauge your audience's comfort level and avoid graphic or intense descriptions unless appropriate.

- **Example:** In a group with people unfamiliar with supernatural topics, begin by summarizing the encounter without heavy details, then offer to share more for those interested in a deeper account.

4. Respect Cultural and Spiritual Beliefs

Supernatural experiences are often tied to cultural and spiritual beliefs, each carrying its own customs, interpretations, and sensitivities. Avoid appropriating or misrepresenting cultural elements that may have specific meanings to certain communities, and refrain from dismissing the validity of other cultural beliefs.

- **Example Statement:** "I'm aware that similar legends exist in different cultures, each with unique interpretations, and I respect the diversity of these beliefs."

Potential Consequences of Sharing Publicly

Sharing supernatural experiences publicly can have both positive and negative consequences. Understanding these potential impacts can help you decide whether, when, and where to share your story.

1. Positive Impact: Building Community and Validation

For many, sharing a supernatural experience can provide validation, reassurance, and a sense of community. Finding others who have had similar experiences can reduce feelings of isolation, helping you integrate the encounter into your personal narrative. Online forums, paranormal groups, or spiritual support communities can offer supportive environments for sharing.

- **Example Outcome:** Joining a paranormal community allows you to share your story with people who have faced similar encounters, building connections that reinforce the validity of your experience.

2. Negative Impact: Skepticism and Dismissal

Not everyone believes in the supernatural, and some individuals may respond with skepticism or dismissal, especially on public platforms. If shared in spaces with mixed beliefs, supernatural experiences may attract critical comments that can be hurtful or invalidating. Considering your emotional readiness for potential pushback can help you decide whether to make your story public.

- **Example Outcome:** Posting on a public blog or social media may attract skeptical comments, which could feel dismissive and discourage further sharing. Moderating comments or limiting where you share can help mitigate this impact.

3. Emotional Vulnerability and Reliving Trauma

Sharing a traumatic or intense experience can reopen old wounds, potentially bringing back feelings of fear, sadness, or vulnerability. If you're sharing publicly, ensure you have coping strategies in place and access to support in case revisiting the encounter brings up challenging emotions.

- **Example Outcome:** Writing a detailed account of the encounter may lead to flashbacks or renewed anxiety, so prepare with grounding exercises and reach out for support as needed.

4. Misinterpretation or Misrepresentation

Once a story is shared publicly, it can be interpreted or shared out of context, leading to potential misinterpretation or misrepresentation of your experience. To avoid misunderstandings, consider using disclaimers or clarifications to outline the intent behind your story and prevent it from being sensationalized.

- **Example:** Add a note to clarify that you're sharing from a personal perspective rather than as an expert or authority on supernatural topics.

5. Impact on Personal Relationships

Friends or family who are skeptical or uncomfortable with supernatural topics may react unexpectedly if you share publicly, potentially leading to tension in relationships. If this is a concern, communicate your reasons for sharing and emphasize that the experience is personal and not meant to challenge others' beliefs.

- **Example Outcome:** Family members might feel uneasy after reading your story. Having a private conversation beforehand, where you explain the reasons for sharing, can help them understand your intentions and support you.

Concluding Thoughts on Sharing Your Story Safely

Sharing an encounter with The Hugging Molly can be an empowering step in processing the experience, finding community, and contributing to the broader discussion of supernatural phenomena. However, sharing also requires sensitivity, respect for diverse beliefs, and consideration of the potential emotional impact on both yourself and your audience. By setting clear intentions, choosing appropriate spaces, and respecting boundaries, you can share your story responsibly, fostering connection, understanding, and empathy.

Remember, how you share is just as important as what you share. A thoughtfully presented story not only respects your own journey but creates a safe space for others, opening doors to compassion, community, and shared human experiences in the mysterious world of the supernatural.

Appendix

Appendix A: Glossary of Terms and Symbols Associated with The Hugging Molly

This glossary provides definitions and explanations of key terms, symbols, and concepts associated with The Hugging Molly. Understanding these terms can enhance your comprehension of her legend, her behaviors, and the cultural context surrounding her encounters. This appendix also includes traditional and supernatural terminology that frequently appears in folklore and paranormal studies, offering a reference for those seeking deeper insights into the lore of The Hugging Molly and similar supernatural figures.

A

Apparition: A visible manifestation of a spirit or ghost. In the case of The Hugging Molly, she is often described as a shadowy apparition that appears suddenly, often in dark or misty settings.

Archetype: In folklore, an archetype is a typical character, symbol, or behavior that represents universal human experiences. The Hugging Molly fits several archetypes, including the "Grieving Mother" and "Guardian of Boundaries," which represent loss, sorrow, and caution.

Aura: A field of energy that surrounds a person or entity. In paranormal beliefs, auras are often visible to those with heightened senses, and they may reveal information about a spirit's intent or emotional state. Witnesses often report a chilling or oppressive aura surrounding The Hugging Molly.

Anxiety Trigger: Any stimulus or situation that provokes anxiety, often linked to a traumatic memory or encounter. For individuals who have encountered The Hugging Molly, certain environmental cues—such as mist, footsteps, or nighttime isolation—can act as triggers that evoke anxiety or fear.

B

Banshee: A supernatural figure in Irish folklore, often depicted as a wailing woman whose cries are a harbinger of death. While not identical, The Hugging Molly's chilling scream is sometimes likened to the banshee's cry, as it instills fear and marks her presence.

Boundary Spirit: A supernatural entity that guards certain areas or limits where the living and the spirit world intersect. The Hugging Molly is sometimes seen as a boundary spirit, as her encounters often occur in transitional or isolated spaces, like pathways and rural outskirts, where she acts as a deterrent.

Bogeyman: A common folklore figure used to caution children against misbehavior, often by instilling fear. The Hugging Molly is sometimes considered a bogeyman-like figure, especially in stories where she acts as a warning to young people to avoid wandering alone at night.

C

Cold Spot: A sudden drop in temperature often associated with the presence of spirits. In encounters with The Hugging Molly, witnesses frequently report experiencing an intense cold, particularly as she draws near, creating an atmosphere that heightens fear.

Cultural Superstitions: Widely held beliefs in certain actions, objects, or behaviors that are believed to have supernatural consequences. The Hugging Molly's story is shaped by cultural superstitions, such as the belief that spirits may seek to enforce social norms or ward off danger.

Curse: A supernatural force believed to bring misfortune to those targeted. While not explicitly part of her behavior, some people interpret The Hugging Molly's scream or embrace as a "curse," although there is no evidence that her encounters cause lasting supernatural harm.

D

Doppelgänger: A spirit or entity that mimics the appearance of a person. While The Hugging Molly is not considered a doppelgänger, her appearance as a human-like figure with eerie, indistinct features often evokes a similar unsettling reaction.

Distress Call: An auditory phenomenon, such as a scream or wail, that serves as a supernatural warning or expression of emotional turmoil. The Hugging Molly's scream, described as haunting and intense, functions as a distress call, alerting people to her presence and adding to the atmosphere of fear.

Divination Tools: Objects used to gain insight into the supernatural, such as pendulums, tarot cards, and scrying mirrors. While these tools are not directly associated with The Hugging Molly, they may be used to interpret or understand her presence and encounters with her.

E

Energy Attachment: A theory that spirits are drawn to individuals or locations with a particular emotional or energetic frequency. The Hugging Molly may be seen as an energy attachment, drawn to those who are alone, vulnerable, or grieving, as her interactions often reflect unresolved sorrow or emotional need.

Entity: A being or force, often used in the context of spirits, ghosts, or supernatural presences. The Hugging Molly is an entity that embodies fear and mystery, often perceived as more than a mere ghost due to her intense interactions with witnesses.

Embrace: The Hugging Molly's signature behavior, in which she envelops an individual in a tight, immobilizing hug. This embrace is interpreted differently depending on the perspective—some see it as protective, others as aggressive, and many as a manifestation of unresolved sorrow.

G

Grieving Mother Archetype: A common figure in folklore, representing a mother who has lost her child and whose spirit roams in search of reconciliation. The Hugging Molly's legend often depicts her as a grieving mother, adding a layer of sympathy to her actions despite her intimidating presence.

Guardian Spirit: A supernatural figure believed to protect individuals or territories. In some interpretations, The Hugging Molly is viewed as a guardian spirit who uses fear to warn travelers of potential danger or to prevent them from wandering into risky areas.

Grounding Technique: A method used to reduce anxiety and remain present, often by focusing on sensory details or physical sensations. After encounters with The Hugging Molly, grounding techniques are recommended to help individuals recover from fear and regain a sense of safety.

H

Haunting: The presence or lingering energy of a spirit or supernatural force in a particular location. The Hugging Molly's appearances are often described as a haunting, as she is seen repeatedly in specific places, such as rural roads or areas of historical significance.

Hypervigilance: A heightened state of alertness often following a traumatic experience. Those who encounter The Hugging Molly may experience hypervigilance, becoming acutely aware of nighttime sounds, shadows, or sudden temperature changes.

I

Imprint Theory: A theory suggesting that intense emotional or traumatic events can leave a residual "imprint" on locations, leading to repeated supernatural occurrences. Some believe The Hugging Molly is an imprint rather than an aware spirit, with her actions replaying as part of a haunting loop.

Intuition: The ability to sense or feel things without logical reasoning, often linked to sensing supernatural presences. Intuition is frequently reported by those who sense The Hugging Molly before they actually see or hear her.

M

Mindfulness: A practice of focusing on the present moment to reduce stress and manage fear. Mindfulness is often recommended as a way to process encounters with The Hugging Molly, as it helps individuals regulate emotions and stay grounded after a frightening experience.

Myth: A traditional story or legend that conveys cultural beliefs, values, or moral lessons. The Hugging Molly's story has evolved as a myth, incorporating elements of caution, fear, and social norms to convey messages about safety and vigilance.

P

Paranormal: Referring to phenomena that cannot be explained by science and are believed to involve supernatural elements. The Hugging Molly's encounters fall under paranormal experiences, as her actions defy conventional understanding and evoke supernatural fear.

Projection Theory: A psychological theory suggesting that individuals may project internal fears or unresolved emotions onto external phenomena, leading to perceived supernatural experiences. This theory is sometimes applied to encounters with The Hugging Molly, suggesting that she may embody suppressed anxieties or grief.

Protective Charm: An object believed to ward off negative energy or supernatural entities, such as amulets, crystals, or symbols. Many carry protective charms when venturing into areas where The Hugging Molly has been seen, seeking a layer of defense against her intense presence.

R

Residual Haunting: A type of haunting where energy from past events replays without an active or aware spirit. Some believe The Hugging Molly's repetitive behavior and appearance in specific locations make her a residual haunting, where her presence is more of an echo than a conscious interaction.

Ritual: A set of actions performed to create a sense of protection, purification, or intention. Some may perform protective rituals before entering areas where The Hugging Molly is rumored to appear, seeking spiritual or emotional safety.

S

Salt Barrier: A line or circle of salt believed to create a protective boundary that spirits cannot cross. Those who encounter The Hugging Molly sometimes carry salt to create a symbolic barrier, intending to protect themselves if they sense her approach.

Skepticism: A critical perspective that questions or doubts supernatural phenomena. Skepticism often arises in discussions of The Hugging Molly, with some viewing her as a psychological construct rather than an actual spirit.

Specter: Another term for a ghost or supernatural figure. The Hugging Molly is frequently referred to as a specter due to her ghostly appearance and the fear she instills.

Spirit Guide: A spirit believed to offer guidance, wisdom, or protection. While not typically considered a spirit guide, some interpretations suggest that The Hugging Molly may serve as a guardian figure warning people of danger through her eerie appearances.

T

Trauma Response: A reaction to a distressing event that may include anxiety, hypervigilance, or emotional numbness. Encounters with The Hugging Molly can provoke trauma responses, as her embrace and scream can be deeply unsettling.

Trigger Warning: A notice that a topic may evoke strong emotional reactions, especially if related to trauma or fear. When sharing stories about The Hugging Molly, trigger warnings can help readers or listeners prepare for potentially distressing content.

V

Vengeful Spirit: A spirit motivated by anger or resentment, often targeting those who have wronged it. While The Hugging Molly is not commonly described as vengeful, some interpretations view her as a protective or punitive figure, particularly toward those who wander in her domain without respect.

Visualization Technique: A mental exercise used to create a sense of safety, calm, or protection. Visualization techniques are often recommended after encountering The Hugging Molly, allowing individuals to mentally create a boundary or protective shield.

W

Wraith: A spectral figure or ghost, typically associated with sorrow or forewarning. The Hugging Molly's spectral presence and emotional intensity can be likened to that of a wraith, embodying grief, mystery, and an element of warning.

Warning Entity: A supernatural figure whose presence or actions serve as a warning to the living. The Hugging Molly's appearances may function as a warning entity, using fear to caution individuals against venturing into unsafe areas alone.

Y

Yurei: In Japanese folklore, a spirit associated with unresolved emotions or grievances, often believed to haunt specific locations. Similar to the Yurei, The Hugging Molly may be motivated by unresolved grief or longing, tethering her to a particular place or set of behaviors.

Concluding Thoughts on Terms and Symbols Associated with The Hugging Molly

This glossary provides a framework for understanding the terminology and symbolism often encountered in discussions about The Hugging Molly. These terms help contextualize her presence within folklore, psychology, and paranormal studies, offering insights into her behavior, motivations, and cultural significance. By exploring these terms, readers gain a deeper appreciation for the legend of The Hugging Molly, as well as the cultural and emotional layers that shape her haunting presence.

Appendix B: Resource List: Experts, Support Groups, and Recommended Reading

The aftermath of a supernatural encounter can leave individuals seeking guidance, support, and knowledge. This appendix offers a comprehensive list of resources, including professionals specializing in trauma and paranormal experiences, support groups for those who've encountered supernatural phenomena, and recommended reading to deepen your understanding of paranormal lore, trauma recovery, and spiritual resilience. These resources are curated to support healing, provide expert insights, and foster community for those processing encounters with figures like The Hugging Molly.

I. Experts in Trauma and Paranormal Studies

Finding the right professionals is essential for processing the emotional and psychological impact of a supernatural encounter. The following categories cover experts specializing in trauma therapy, paranormal research, and supernatural psychology.

1. Trauma Therapists and Counselors

Trauma therapists are mental health professionals trained to support individuals dealing with fear, anxiety, and post-traumatic stress. Seeking a therapist with experience in supernatural or traumatic experiences can help you process encounters in a non-judgmental setting.

- **EMDR (Eye Movement Desensitization and Reprocessing) Therapists:** EMDR is an effective technique for trauma recovery, helping individuals reprocess distressing memories. To find certified EMDR therapists, visit:
    - EMDR International Association (EMDRIA): https://www.emdria.org
    - EMDR Institute: https://emdr.com
- **Certified Trauma Specialists:**

- ◦ **Psychology Today's Therapist Directory**: This directory allows you to filter for therapists specializing in trauma and anxiety, and you can search by location for in-person or virtual sessions. https://www.psychologytoday.com/us/therapists
- ◦ **National Center for PTSD**: Resources and referrals for finding specialized trauma care, including support for veterans and civilians. https://www.ptsd.va.gov

2. Paranormal Psychologists

Paranormal psychology is a field that examines supernatural experiences from a psychological perspective, aiming to understand how individuals interpret and process these phenomena. Specialists in paranormal psychology can provide insights that bridge the gap between science and the supernatural.

- **Parapsychological Association:** An international organization that promotes scientific study of paranormal phenomena. Their directory of researchers and psychologists includes experts who may be able to offer consultations. https://parapsych.org
- **Rhine Research Center:** Focused on parapsychological studies, including experiences of haunting, ESP, and apparitions. The center offers resources, educational materials, and events on paranormal psychology. https://www.rhineonline.org

3. Spiritual Counselors and Intuitive Healers

Spiritual counselors and intuitive healers can offer non-traditional support, especially if the encounter with The Hugging Molly has left a lingering sense of fear or spiritual unrest. Many individuals find comfort in exploring these practices.

- **American Association of Psychics**: Provides a directory of psychics and spiritual counselors specializing in paranormal and supernatural matters. These professionals can offer emotional guidance, energy readings, and insights for processing supernatural encounters. https://americanassociationofpsychics.com

- **The International Association of Reiki Professionals (IARP)**: A directory of certified Reiki healers and energy workers trained to help with emotional and spiritual healing, useful for those seeking balance after a supernatural experience. https://iarp.org

II. Support Groups and Online Communities

Support groups and online communities provide a safe, understanding environment to share experiences, gain validation, and connect with others who have encountered similar supernatural events.

1. Supernatural and Paranormal Support Groups

- **International Paranormal Society (IPS):** A global organization offering both online and in-person support for individuals who have had paranormal experiences. They provide forums, events, and discussion groups for sharing stories and receiving support. https://www.internationalparanormalsociety.org
- **Ghost Research Society (GRS):** Based in the United States, GRS offers resources, case studies, and community events. They also have a Facebook group for members to share experiences, ask questions, and seek advice. https://www.ghostresearch.org
- **Paranormal Network on Reddit:** An active online community where users share their paranormal encounters and discuss theories, coping methods, and support. Relevant subreddits include:
    - **r/Paranormal**: A general forum for all paranormal experiences.
    - **r/Ghosts**: Dedicated to ghost sightings and supernatural stories.

2. Mental Health Support Groups for Trauma and Anxiety

For those dealing with the psychological aftermath of a supernatural experience, mental health support groups provide emotional support and practical coping strategies.

- **Anxiety and Depression Association of America (ADAA):** Offers support group listings for those managing trauma, fear, and anxiety, as well as an online support community. https://adaa.org
- **Mental Health America (MHA):** Provides a directory of local support groups for anxiety, PTSD, and trauma recovery. https://mhanational.org
- **7 Cups of Tea:** A peer support network offering free online chat with trained listeners, as well as support groups for anxiety, fear, and post-trauma recovery. https://www.7cups.com

3. Spiritual and Religious Support Groups

For individuals seeking a faith-based approach to processing supernatural experiences, spiritual support groups offer community and encouragement within a religious or spiritual context.

- **Spiritual Emergence Network (SEN):** A nonprofit organization dedicated to supporting those experiencing spiritual crises, including encounters with the supernatural. They offer referrals to counselors and resources for spiritual support. https://www.spiritualemergence.org
- **Faith-Based Support in Local Places of Worship:** Many churches, synagogues, mosques, and temples offer pastoral counseling and faith-based support groups for individuals coping with supernatural or traumatic experiences. Check with local places of worship for available support options.

III. Recommended Reading

Reading about folklore, paranormal phenomena, trauma recovery, and resilience can help contextualize your experience, offering tools and perspectives that support healing and understanding.

1. Books on Paranormal Phenomena and Folklore

- **"Ghostland: An American History in Haunted Places" by Colin Dickey** – This book explores haunted sites across America and delves into the cultural impact of ghost stories. It's an insightful read for understanding how stories like The Hugging Molly's fit into broader folklore traditions.

- **"The Encyclopedia of Ghosts and Spirits" by Rosemary Ellen Guiley** – A comprehensive reference book covering various supernatural entities, including figures similar to The Hugging Molly. This guide provides historical, cultural, and symbolic perspectives on supernatural phenomena.

- **"Real Ghosts, Restless Spirits, and Haunted Places" by Brad Steiger** – An anthology of ghostly encounters, legends, and hauntings that examines common themes in paranormal experiences and the impact of these stories on society.

2. Books on Coping with Trauma and Fear

- **"The Body Keeps the Score: Brain, Mind, and Body in the Healing of Trauma" by Dr. Bessel van der Kolk** – A foundational text for understanding how trauma affects the body and mind, offering strategies for healing and resilience.

- **"Waking the Tiger: Healing Trauma" by Dr. Peter A. Levine** – This book provides insight into how trauma is processed in the body and offers somatic exercises for releasing fear and tension. It's a practical guide for those recovering from any intense, fear-inducing encounter.

- **"Anxiety: The Missing Stage of Grief" by Claire Bidwell Smith** – This book explores the connection between anxiety and grief, offering coping mechanisms and insights that may help those dealing with lingering fear or sorrow from an encounter.

3. Books on Building Spiritual Resilience and Protection

- **"Psychic Self-Defense: The Classic Instruction Manual for Protecting Yourself Against Paranormal Attack" by Dion Fortune** – Written by an experienced occultist, this book offers techniques for spiritual and psychic protection, useful for anyone feeling vulnerable after a supernatural encounter.

- **"The Power of Now: A Guide to Spiritual Enlightenment" by Eckhart Tolle** – Tolle's book on mindfulness and presence can help individuals reclaim peace and reduce fear, focusing on grounding and emotional resilience.

- **"Sacred Woman: A Guide to Healing the Feminine Body, Mind, and Spirit" by Queen Afua** – This book provides a guide to spiritual healing through rituals, affirmations, and practices designed to empower resilience, especially useful for those processing supernatural encounters that leave an emotional impact.

IV. Online Articles and Resources

For accessible information on trauma recovery, paranormal studies, and folklore, the following websites and articles offer a wealth of free resources.

- **PsychCentral:** An online resource with articles on coping with anxiety, trauma, and supernatural experiences. https://psychcentral.com
- **The Folklore Society:** A UK-based organization offering articles, publications, and resources on folklore, including studies on supernatural figures like The Hugging Molly. https://folklore-society.com
- **Mental Health Foundation's Anxiety and Trauma Resource Page:** Offers downloadable guides on coping with anxiety, PTSD, and fear-based experiences. https://mentalhealth.org.uk
- **American Folklore:** A website dedicated to American folklore and paranormal stories, featuring articles and folklore resources relevant to understanding figures like The Hugging Molly. https://americanfolklore.net

Concluding Thoughts on Resources for Support and Understanding

The journey to recovery and understanding after an encounter with The Hugging Molly—or any supernatural experience—can benefit greatly from reliable support, informed guidance, and community connection. This resource list offers multiple avenues for seeking help, understanding, and camaraderie, whether through professional expertise, peer support, or self-directed reading.

Processing and healing from such an experience is a deeply personal journey, but with the resources outlined here, you can take empowered steps toward resilience, self-awareness, and a sense of peace. Remember that you are not alone on this journey; there are supportive networks and compassionate professionals ready to assist, allowing you to integrate the experience into a stronger, more balanced self.

<u>Message from the Author:</u>

I hope you enjoyed this book, I love astrology and knew there was not a book such as this out on the shelf. I love metaphysical items as well. Please check out my other books:

-Life of Government Benefits

-My life of Hell

-My life with Hydrocephalus

-Red Sky

-World Domination:Woman's rule

-World Domination:Woman's Rule 2: The War

-Life and Banishment of Apophis: book 1

-The Kidney Friendly Diet

-The Ultimate Hemp Cookbook

-Creating a Dispensary(legally)

-Cleanliness throughout life: the importance of showering from childhood to adulthood.

-Strong Roots: The Risks of Overcoddling children

-Hemp Horoscopes: Cosmic Insights and Earthly Healing

- Celestial Hemp Navigating the Zodiac: Through the Green Cosmos

-Astrological Hemp: Aligning The Stars with Earth's Ancient Herb

-The Astrological Guide to Hemp: Stars, Signs, and Sacred Leaves

-Green Growth: Innovative Marketing Strategies for your Hemp Products and Dispensary

-Cosmic Cannabis

-Astrological Munchies

-Henry The Hemp

-Zodiacal Roots: The Astrological Soul Of Hemp

- **Green Constellations: Intersection of Hemp and Zodiac**

-Hemp in The Houses: An astrological Adventure Through The Cannabis Galaxy

-Galactic Ganja Guide

Heavenly Hemp

Zodiac Leaves

Doctor Who Astrology

Cannastrology

Stellar Satvias and Cosmic Indicas

Celestial Cannabis: A Zodiac Journey

AstroHerbology: The Sky and The Soil: Volume 1

AstroHerbology:Celestial Cannabis:Volume 2

Cosmic Cannabis Cultivation

The Starry Guide to Herbal Harmony: Volume 1

The Starry Guide to Herbal Harmony: Cannabis Universe: Volume 2

Yugioh Astrology: Astrological Guide to Deck, Duels and more

Nightmare Mansion: Echoes of The Abyss

Nightmare Mansion 2: Legacy of Shadows

Nightmare Mansion 3: Shadows of the Forgotten

Nightmare Mansion 4: Echoes of the Damned

The Life and Banishment of Apophis: Book 2

Nightmare Mansion: Halls of Despair

Healing with Herb: Cannabis and Hydrocephalus

Planetary Pot: Aligning with Astrological Herbs: Volume 1

Fast Track to Freedom: 30 Days to Financial Independence Using AI, Assets, and Agile Hustles

Cosmic Hemp Pathways

How to Become Financially Free in 30 Days: 10,000 Paths to Prosperity

Zodiacal Herbage: Astrological Insights: Volume 1

Nightmare Mansion: Whispers in the Walls

The Daleks Invade Atlantis

Henry the hemp and Hydrocephalus

10X The Kidney Friendly Diet
Cannabis Universe: Adult coloring book
Hemp Astrology: The Healing Power of the Stars
Zodiacal Herbage: Astrological Insights: Cannabis Universe: Volume 2
<u>**Planetary Pot: Aligning with Astrological Herbs: Cannabis Universes: Volume 2**</u>
Doctor Who Meets the Replicators and SG-1: The Ultimate Battle for Survival
Nightmare Mansion: Curse of the Blood Moon
<u>**The Celestial Stoner: A Guide to the Zodiac**</u>
Cosmic Pleasures: Sex Toy Astrology for Every Sign
Hydrocephalus Astrology: Navigating the Stars and Healing Waters
Lapis and the Mischievous Chocolate Bar

Celestial Positions: Sexual Astrology for Every Sign
Apophis's Shadow Work Journal: : A Journey of Self-Discovery and Healing
Kinky Cosmos: Sexual Kink Astrology for Every Sign
Digital Cosmos: The Astrological Digimon Compendium
Stellar Seeds: The Cosmic Guide to Growing with Astrology
Apophis's Daily Gratitude Journal

Cat Astrology: Feline Mysteries of the Cosmos
The Cosmic Kama Sutra: An Astrological Guide to Sexual Positions
Unleash Your Potential: A Guided Journal Powered by AI Insights
Whispers of the Enchanted Grove

Cosmic Pleasures: An Astrological Guide to Sexual Kinks

369, 12 Manifestation Journal

Whisper of the nocturne journal(blank journal for writing or drawing)

The Boogey Book

Locked In Reflection: A Chastity Journey Through Locktober

Generating Wealth Quickly:

How to Generate $100,000 in 24 Hours

Star Magic: Harness the Power of the Universe

The Flatulence Chronicles: A Fart Journal for Self-Discovery

The Doctor and The Death Moth

Seize the Day: A Personal Seizure Tracking Journal

The Ultimate Boogeyman Safari: A Journey into the Boogie World and Beyond

Whispers of Samhain: 1,000 Spells of Love, Luck, and Lunar Magic: Samhain Spell Book

Apophis's guides:

Witch's Spellbook Crafting Guide for Halloween

<u>Frost & Flame: The Enchanted Yule Grimoire of 1000 Winter Spells</u>

<u>The Ultimate Boogey Goo Guide & Spooky Activities for Halloween Fun</u>

Harmony of the Scales: A Libra's Spellcraft for Balance and Beauty

The Enchanted Advent: 36 Days of Christmas Wonders

Nightmare Mansion: The Labyrinth of Screams

Harvest of Enchantment: 1,000 Spells of Gratitude, Love, and Fortune for Thanksgiving

The Boogey Chronicles: A Journal of Nightly Encounters and Shadowy Secrets

The 12 Days of Financial Freedom: A Step-by-Step Christmas Countdown to Transform Your Finances

Sigil of the Eternal Spiral Blank Journal

A Christmas Feast: Timeless Recipes for Every Meal

Holiday Stress-Free Solutions: A Survival Guide to Thriving During the Festive Season

Yu-Gi-Oh! Holiday Gifting Mastery: The Ultimate Guide for Fans and Newcomers Alike

Holiday Harmony: A Hydrocephalus Survival Guide for the Festive Season

Celestial Craft: The Witch's Almanac for 2025 – A Cosmic Guide to Manifestations, Moons, and Mystical Events

Doctor Who: The Toymaker's Winter Wonderland

Tulsa King Unveiled: A Thrilling Guide to Stallone's Mafia Masterpiece

Pendulum Craft: A Complete Guide to Crafting and Using Personalized Divination Tools

Nightmare Mansion: Santa's Eternal Eve

Starlight Noel: A Cosmic Journey through Christmas Mysteries

The Dark Architect: Unlocking the Blueprint of Existence

If you want solar for your home go here: https://www.harborso-lar.live/apophisenterprises/

Get Some Tarot cards: https://www.makeplayingcards.com/sell/apophis-occult-shop

Get   some   shirts: https://www.bonfire.com/store/apophis-shirt-emporium/

<u>Instagrams:</u>
@apophis_enterprises,
@apophisbookemporium,
@apophisscardshop
Twitter: @apophisenterpr1 Tiktok:@apophisenterprise
Youtube: @sg1fan23477, @FiresideRetreatKingdom
Hive: @sg1fan23477
CheeLee: @SG1fan23477

Podcast: Apophis Chat Zone: https://open.spotify.com/show/5zXbrCLEV2xzCp8ybrfHsk?si=fb4d4fdbdce44dec

Newsletter: https://apophiss-newsletter-27c897.beehiiv.com/